MAD

HOW TO DEAL WITH YOUR ANGER AND GET RESPECT

James J. Crist, Ph.D.

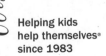

free spirit
PUBLiSHiNG®

Helping kids
help themselves®
since 1983

Cataloging-in-Publication Data
Crist, James J.
  Mad : how to deal with your anger and get respect / James J. Crist.
     p. cm.
  Includes bibliographical references and index.
  ISBN-13: 978-1-57542-267-1
  ISBN-10: 1-57542-267-0
  1. Anger in adolescence. 2. Teenagers—Conduct of life. I. Title.
  BF724.3.A55C75 2007
  155.5'1247—dc22

                                                                          2007028431

Edited by Eric Braun
Cover design by Marieka Heinlen
Interior design by Marieka Heinlen and Natasha Kenyon
Illustrations by Natasha Kenyon

10 9 8 7 6 5 4 3 2 1
Printed in the United States of America

Free Spirit Publishing Inc.
217 Fifth Avenue North, Suite 200
Minneapolis, MN 55401-1299
(612) 338-2068
help4kids@freespirit.com
www.freespirit.com

Free Spirit Publishing is a member of the Green Press Initiative, and we're committed to printing our books on recycled paper containing a minimum of 30% post-consumer waste (PCW). For every ton of books printed on 30% PCW recycled paper, we save 5.1 trees, 2,100 gallons of water, 114 gallons of oil, 18 pounds of air pollution, 1,230 kilowatt hours of energy, and .9 cubic yards of landfill space. At Free Spirit it's our goal to nurture not only young people, but nature too!

green press INITIATIVE

Dedication

I dedicate this book to all the young people for whom anger control is a problem. Anger causes so many problems in relationships with others. It is my hope that by sharing what I have learned about getting a handle on your anger, you can control it before it controls you.

Acknowledgments

I'd like to thank my editor, Eric Braun, for his help in revising my book and making it easier to read. Thanks to Marieka Heinlen and Tasha Kenyon for their design and artwork—you do such a great job! I'd like to thank all of my friends, family members, and colleagues for sharing their feedback on the book title and cover design—it's always helpful to hear a variety of perspectives. Thanks also to Thomas S. Greenspon, Ph.D., for reading and commenting on the manuscript. And I would like to thank everyone at Free Spirit for their continued support of my work and for making the process so much easier.

Finally, I would like to thank my patients and other teens who have shared their stories of anger with me. Your courage in facing your anger has inspired me to write this book and will help many more teens face theirs. Dealing with anger takes practice, but it's worth the effort when you can put your anger into words and get the respect you want and deserve.

CONTENTS

INTRODUCTION: ANGER IS LIKE A FIRE

I'm so angry about events at school that it's hard for me to concentrate on classwork and homework. I've grabbed a few kids. A girl made a negative comment to me, so I told her, "Do you want to be on my list, too?" School officials assumed I had made a "hit list," which isn't true. I just said it to scare her, but I can understand why she felt threatened.

I'm also having trouble with one of the guys in my class. He keeps ticking me off, giving me weird looks and making annoying noises. I assumed his face was telling me, "You're a crazy weirdo." He told me no one cared about me, which really upset me. —Boy, 13

People who mess with me make me mad. I just feel like leaving to go by myself a little while until I'm not as angry. If I'm really mad I just go punch a wall or something. —Boy, 16

When I'm mad I trash things. I throw things. I talk to people, too, and listen to music to give myself some time to think rationally.

I have been hurt by my own anger. I said some things I didn't mean to say, and it caused a person I care about to leave my life. —Girl, 18

1

> Anger feels horrible. I hate being mad! I think of a way that I could make things better. Sometimes I get so mad I will punch the wall or something, but not someone.
> —Girl, 13

Have you ever felt so mad about something that you were ready to explode? Or maybe you did explode. Say someone at school insults you or shoves you. Who wouldn't get angry and want to push back? Have you ever wanted to go out with friends and your dad tells you no, without giving you a good reason? Storming out of the room and slamming a door or two might seem like a normal thing to do. Maybe you yell at your dad and argue with him. You hope to change his mind. But in your anger, you say some hurtful things and get yourself into more trouble. This just makes you madder.

Everyone gets angry sometimes. It's a normal human feeling. For most people, anger comes and then goes. They don't lash out or hold onto anger for too long. But some people have a hard time controlling their anger. They might blow up over little things or hold a grudge for a long time. They might say things that damage their relationships.

Anger can even lead to violence or trouble with the law. In 2005 alone, law enforcement agencies in the United States arrested about 95,300 teens for violent crimes, such as assault and robbery. Those arrests made up about 16 percent (16 out of every 100) of all violent crime arrests that year. Many teens commit crimes out of anger and frustration. In a few extreme cases, teens are even mad enough to kill.

Maybe you know how it feels to be this mad. Maybe you have trouble controlling your anger. If you're like most teens, you want to be heard. You want respect. But when your anger is out of control, it's hard for people to take you seriously. They focus on the hurtful ways you express your anger instead of on the reasons you have to be mad (even though they may be good reasons). Basically, you *lose* people's respect.

You may even have trouble respecting yourself.

In many ways, anger is like a fire. You can add fuel to your anger, so it rages and who knows what will be destroyed. Or you can keep it under control and let it burn out. And just like fire, you can even use anger in positive ways. You can let it shine light on a problem you need to fix.

Even if it seems like your anger controls you sometimes, there *are* things you can do. You don't have to get in trouble. You don't have to let your relationships get hurt. You have the power to take charge of your anger. When you do, you'll feel better. Your relationships will be stronger, and you'll even be physically healthier.

This book can help you take charge of your anger. I'm a psychologist, and I've helped hundreds of kids who had problems with anger. I wrote this book so I can help you, too. Controlling anger can be hard to do. After all, you have real reasons to be mad. Sometimes it may seem like nobody understands that. People may tell you not to get mad, but that's not fair. We all get angry sometimes. But *controlling* your anger is up to you and only you.

WHAT'S IN THIS BOOK

Mad is divided into four parts:

- Part 1 is **The Truth About Anger.** You'll learn where anger comes from, why it's so hard for many teens to control it, and how to tell how much of a problem you have with anger.

- Part 2 is **Tame the Flames.** You'll learn the difference between healthy and not-so-healthy ways to express your anger; you'll find tools you can use to help control your anger; and you'll learn lifestyle choices that help you feel angry less often and less intensely.

- Part 3 is **Anger and Relationships.** You'll learn how anger affects family, romantic, and friend relationships; why anger can be so intense in relationships; and how to keep respect at the forefront, so your relationships stay healthy and positive.

- Part 4 is **Burning Issues.** You'll learn about disorders that can make your anger problems worse and/or harder to control; you'll find out about the legal system (in case anger gets you into trouble with the law); and you'll learn how counseling can help you get your anger under control.

You will get the most out of this book if you read all of it. But feel free to skip around if that's more your style. For example, if your anger is causing problems with your dad, you can check out Chapter 7 (The Fire at Home: Anger in Families). If you've gotten in trouble with the law, you might want to start with Chapter 11 (When Anger Gets You in Trouble). How you use this book is up to you. Every chapter provides useful information and help.

This book also has stories and quotes from real teens in every chapter. Names have been removed to protect privacy, but the words are real. As you read them, think about what these teens say. Do their anger issues sound like yours? Have you ever been in situations like theirs? If so, what did you do? If not, what would you do if you were?

Learning to control your anger is hard, but remember: Lots of teens have overcome their problems with anger, and so can you. You have to work at it. If you're reading this book, you've already shown you have the courage needed.

I'd like to know how this book has helped you or if you have any questions about controlling your anger. Feel free to email me at help4kids@freespirit.com or send a letter to me in care of:

Free Spirit Publishing
217 Fifth Avenue North, Suite 200
Minneapolis, MN 55401-1299

Be sure to include your address, so I can write back to you.

Dr. James J. Crist

PART 1
THE TRUTH ABOUT ANGER

EVERYONE GETS MAD

I was teased a lot by two classmates when I was in school. They would call me a "fat-ass white boy" all the time. I hate it when people judge me for the way I look instead of who I am. A lot of times I felt like beating the living sh** out of them or chucking a rock at them. In my head, I'd call them the n-word, even though I hate the idea of being racist and the two people in my class who did accept me for who I am were black—one of whom is still my best friend. I know the race issue had nothing to do with it, but when I'd get ticked off it was hard not to feel that way.
—Boy, 18

What makes me angry is my uncle stealing from me.
—Girl, 17

People who make fun of my mom make me mad. —Boy, 17

My dad has pushed me around before and yelled a lot at me because he's angry. —Girl, 15

I get mad when I see animals like dogs getting abused. —Boy, 15

Anger hurts, like my stomach drops. I can't think straight. I want to yell. I cry when it gets out of control and crying really controls it. —Girl, 16

When I'm mad my hands get shaky and I get nervous. And it feels like even though you know there's people who love you, at that moment if feels like no one knows how you feel. —Girl, 15

Anger is a feeling. It's not anything you do or say, or anything that happens. Most of the time you don't have much choice in whether you feel it. Anger is not good or bad. This is important: **Everyone has a right to get angry.** How else should you feel when you are hurt or threatened? Think of anger as a warning signal. It means something isn't right and you need to take some action.

You may not be able to control when you get mad, or how mad you get. But there's something you *can* control. You can control how you react to anger. If you react to anger in unhealthy ways, you can

- damage relationships
- risk your future
- get in trouble with the law
- hurt yourself
- put a lot of stress on your body

So you can see that controlling your reaction to anger is really important! You can start improving your anger control by figuring out what makes you mad.

The Physical Cost of Anger

Anger is harmful for your body. Studies have shown that men who show high levels of anger and hostility are twice as likely to have a heart attack compared to people who tend to stay calm.

Problems expressing anger (either stuffing it inside or blowing up) also can cause high blood pressure. Why is this? When you are angry, your body releases a brain chemical, norepinephrine (NO-ruh-pi-NEFF-rin), that energizes you so you are ready to protect yourself from physical harm. Norepinephrine tends to make your blood vessels narrower. It's like stepping on a garden hose: the pressure of the water inside increases. When this happens in your body, your blood pressure rises. High blood pressure raises your risk of having a heart attack or a stroke, which can cause lasting brain damage. Holding onto anger for long periods of time can also cause headaches and stomachaches. If you have a condition such as asthma, anger can make it worse.

You might think you don't need to worry about these problems until you are older. But these problems can start well before you become an adult. Researchers recently found a strong connection between anger problems and negative changes in the arteries of school-age children. In other studies, young men who react to stress with anger were three times as likely to develop heart disease. They were five times as likely to have a heart attack when compared with others who were calmer.

My problems started when my parents didn't get along and decided to get divorced. I'm the oldest of four in my family and I felt I had to look out for my siblings. My parents would confide in me, which just added to my stress and frustration. My mom would cry about how bad my dad was, and my dad would defend himself and try to win me over. They even wanted me to go to court with them, each of them thinking that I'd help their case. I didn't think I was angry, but I started developing bad stomachaches and got depressed to the point of having suicidal thoughts. I saw a doctor who told me my stomachaches were caused by stress. I started missing school because I was too sick to go, which really ticked off my dad. He got on my case all the time about my grades and missing assignments. The more he pestered me, the less I felt like trying, and I started failing. —Boy, 17

WHAT GETS YOU ANGRY?

Anger is not an all-or-nothing feeling, though sometimes it can seem that way. It can range from mild irritation to explosive rage. The intensity of a person's anger usually depends on what triggers it. For example, you might feel irritated if someone bumps into you in the hallway or if your plans to get together with friends fall through. You might feel more angry if your teacher gets on your case for being late to class when you think it wasn't your fault. And you might feel enraged if someone threatens you physically or you are falsely accused of cheating on your girlfriend or boyfriend.

Here's what a few teens had to say about what makes them mad.

My parents piss me off. They have Ph.D.s in pissing me off. They're really strict and I get grounded for everything I do. I can't breathe without them grounding me for something.—*Girl*, 15

Being teased.—*Boy*, 15

Boys picking on people or calling people names. —*Girl*, 16

Hypocrites, procrastination, chewing with your mouth open, intolerance, discrimination, and harassment.—*Boy*, 15

My girlfriend and I have been arguing for a long time. First she tells me she wants to "take a break" from the relationship and figure things out. Then she starts calling me to get together, and now I'm really confused. We had it out last week—I lost control and punched the siding of the house. Now there's a big dent in it and my parents tell me I have to fix it. I know I'd never lay a hand on a girl, but my parents tell me that I might get a reputation for being violent, and what girl's parents are going to want me to date their daughter? I don't think I ever would, but I kind of see where they're coming from.—**Boy, 18**

Here are some other common anger triggers. You can probably add a few of your own.

- Your mom yells at you.
- Your dad says no to something you want or want to do.
- Friends or peers tease you or insult you.
- Someone puts down someone you care about.
- Someone lies to you or cheats you.
- Someone cuts you off while you're driving.
- Someone pushes you in the hallway at school.
- You get detention for being late to class.
- Someone breaks or takes something important to you.

Journal Your Anger Triggers

Writing down your thoughts and feelings in a journal is a great way to learn about how you deal with anger. It helps you see if things you're doing might be hurting others or yourself. Keep writing. Over time, as you work on getting better at controlling your anger, your journal can help you keep track of your progress. Look for journal boxes like this one throughout this book for ideas on what to write about.

You don't have to write a lot. A few sentences for each entry is enough. Even just a handful of words can help. If you're not into journaling, you can use the journal prompts in this book as ideas for drawing pictures or talking to someone who cares.

You can start your journal by listing things that tick you off. Maybe some of the things on the list on page 12 will be on your list. What else would you add? After you've got a few anger triggers on your list, put a checkmark next to the ones that *really* make you mad. Finally, pick one of those triggers and write about a time when it happened. Why do you think it made you so mad?

Thoughts or beliefs can also trigger anger. Here are some examples. Can you think of others?

- You think your girlfriend or boyfriend is cheating on you.

- You believe your parents treat your siblings better than they treat you.

- When others laugh, you think they are laughing at you.

- When you struggle with homework that seems too hard, you think the teacher is out to get you.

- You think you don't measure up to others in some way; you're jealous of people you think are better than you.

Deeper Sources of Anger

People who have been abused—physically, verbally, emotionally, or sexually—are likely to have a lot of anger held inside. So are people who grow up in unsafe or unstable homes. Examples of this include homes where there is a lot of violence, or where the adults are abusing drugs or alcohol. It's normal to feel angry when those who are supposed to love you and take care of you don't do a good job. It can also feel confusing, because you may still care about the people who abused you, yet you feel angry at them at the same time. And since letting them know how you feel may lead to more abuse, you keep your anger inside.

People who have anger because of abuse might not know how much anger they are carrying until something else triggers it. They may overreact to something small and struggle to understand why they got so mad.

For example, if a parent has abused you verbally, and then your girlfriend yells at you for something, you may fly off the handle at her. You might be surprised at all the anger that comes out. Your girlfriend probably wasn't trying to hurt you, but your pent-up anger caused you to explode.

If you have been abused or are being abused, or if you don't feel safe in your home, talk to an adult you trust right away. You deserve to be safe. There are hotlines you can call if you don't know who you can trust. You can call the National Center for Victims of Crime at 1-800-FYI-CALL (1-800-394-2255) or the National Domestic Violence Hotline at 1-800-799-SAFE (1-800-799-7233). It might seem hard to know what to say. It's usually best to be simple and direct. You could say:

- "I need your help."
- "I'm scared. My dad's abusing me."
- "I have a problem. Can you help me?"

The hotline counselor will need to know basic information about you—age, address, and details about the abuse and the abuser. Within 24 to 48 hours of your call, someone from the agency will talk with you at your school or home. If you're afraid to have the workers visit your home, tell them so. They can visit you at school and place you somewhere safe right away.

WHAT DO YOU DO WITH YOUR ANGER?

For some people, it takes a lot to get them angry. They may be naturally easygoing and find that most things don't get to them. When they do get mad, they don't blow up. This doesn't make them better—it just means that they don't have problems with anger.

For other people, anger bubbles to the surface more often and more intensely. They may also have trouble letting go of their anger—they keep thinking about the situation, which makes it worse. People who feel anger this way often react by becoming aggressive, either verbally or physically. Yelling or name-calling are verbal reactions to anger. Throwing things, breaking things, or hitting things or people, including yourself, are physical reactions. Aggressive responses like this can cause harm to others as well as to yourself.

Check out how the following teens react to their anger. Do any of these responses sound familiar to you?

When I get mad, my body feels like it's on fire. The thoughts that go through my head are that I want to hurt them, the people who made me mad.—Boy, 17

Once, I pulled this girl's hair out.—Girl, 14

I get really angry with my brother. He makes noises or whistles, or does things that annoy me on purpose. I usually try to ignore him, but that doesn't always work. I feel my anger gradually building up. I'll yell at him if he won't stop. Sometimes I hit or push him—he tells my mom, who then restricts me from playing video games. I know I could have handled it better, but it's hard.—*Boy, 13*

Some people express their anger by being **passive-aggressive.** This means they show their anger indirectly, so they don't have to admit they're mad. One of the most common examples is forgetting to do something they don't really want to do. Instead of being open about not wanting to do it, they agree to do it but then "forget." Another example of passive-aggressive anger is being late. By being late, they can upset the people they're mad at without admitting they are mad.

I take my anger out on other people by not talking to them.—*Girl, 13*

Journal What Do You Do When You're Mad?

You've taken a close look at what makes you mad, and you're willing to try to change. The next step is taking a look at what you *do* when you're mad. Think about a time when you were mad recently, and write about it. (You can draw pictures if you prefer, or talk about these ideas with someone you're close to and whom you trust.) Describe what happened that made you mad, and then answer these questions:

- How did your body let you know you were angry?
- What thoughts went through your head while your anger was building?
- How did you express it (what did you do to release your anger)?
- How did it affect the person you were angry at, or took out your anger on? What happened as a result?
- What do you think the other person's goal was? Was he or she trying to upset you on purpose? What message was the person giving you?
- How do you feel about it now? Are you satisfied with how it turned out?

If things didn't turn out well, what would you have liked to happen instead? Write about what you could have done differently to get a different result.

Even if it's tough for you, it's up to you to make sure no one gets hurt as a result of your anger. It's *your* anger. You can choose to take responsibility for it.

2

YOUR BRAIN IS BUILT FOR ANGER

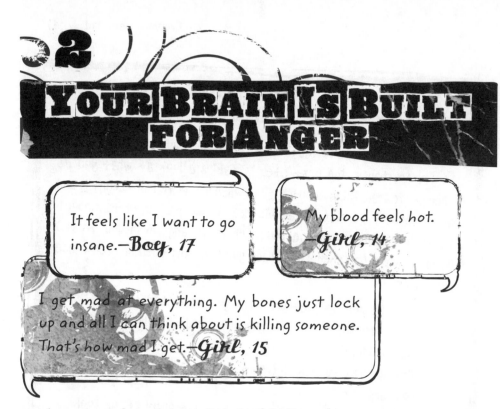

It feels like I want to go insane.—Boy, 17

My blood feels hot. —Girl, 14

I get mad at everything. My bones just lock up and all I can think about is killing someone. That's how mad I get.—Girl, 15

Anger can be an overwhelming feeling for anyone. For many people, it seems like more than just an emotion—they can feel it in their bodies. People do things when they're angry that they normally wouldn't do.

For teens, it can be even more overwhelming. One reason is you're growing into a young man or woman, and you want to make more of your own decisions. But you still have lots of people telling you what to do, like parents and teachers. That can lead to a lot of stress and anger.

Another reason is the way your brain is developing. Psychologists used to think that your brain was done developing by the time you reached your teenage years. But now they know that's not true. Actually, it's often not until people are in their mid-twenties that their brain is finally mature. The way your brain develops during your teen years explains why your emotions, like anger, can feel so intense. It also explains why they can be so hard to control. You may have a lot of trouble controlling your anger *just because you're a teen!*

Journal **How Does It Feel When You're Mad?**

How does it feel when you get really mad? Can you feel it in your body? Maybe in your hands or head? Does your heart race? Does it feel like your eyes are on fire? Write, draw, or talk about how your body feels when you get mad. Think of these as your **anger warning signs.**

YOUR BRAIN AND ANGER

The cerebrum (or cerebral cortex) is what most people think of as the brain. In humans, it is the largest part of the brain. It's divided down the middle into two hemispheres, or halves. Each hemisphere is made up of four main lobes, or sections: the frontal lobe, the temporal lobe, the parietal lobe, and the occipital lobe.

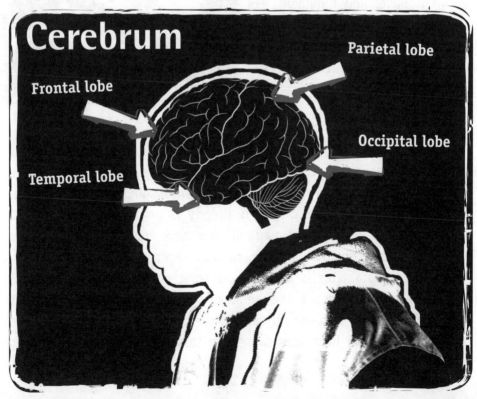

Cerebrum

Parietal lobe

Frontal lobe

Occipital lobe

Temporal lobe

Anger, like all emotions, involves many parts of the brain. But a group of brain structures called the **limbic system** plays a central role. Part of the limbic system is located in the temporal lobes, and parts of the system are located outside the cerebrum. None of the system is located at the front of the brain.

The **frontal lobes** are what people use to control their anger. These are located at the front of the brain. The frontal lobes are responsible for things like thinking, language, and judgment. For example, you use your frontal lobes when you imagine what might be the consequences of your actions.

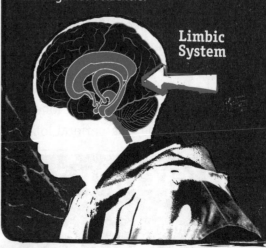

The "Reptilian Brain"

The limbic system in humans is sometimes called the "reptilian brain." That's because more primitive animals, such as reptiles and lower mammals, have a similar limbic system. This part of the brain controls basic body functions such as temperature, breathing, and survival instincts. Imagine how a reptile might think. Most of a reptile's existence is concerned with eating, reproducing, and defending itself against attackers.

Limbic System

Brain Development

So how does being a teenager make it harder to control your anger? A big reason is because the frontal lobes are the last part of the brain to mature. While a teenager's frontal lobes are still developing, his or her limbic system already is producing emotions. At times, the frontal lobes may not be mature enough to control your reactions to strong emotions, such as anger.

Another factor is hormones. During puberty the brain begins releasing hormones. These chemicals control your growth and development. They also can influence your mood and how easily excited you get. Your hormones cause you to seek out new and exciting situations. Meanwhile, the control centers of the brain (the frontal lobes) are not yet fully functioning. As a result, you may end up venting your anger because it feels good without thinking about the consequences first.

Important! None of this means you can use your brain or your hormones as an excuse for losing control. It's true that these things can make it harder to control your anger. But you are still responsible for how you choose to handle your anger. Most teens do a good job dealing with their anger—you can, too!

Neurotransmitters

Brain chemicals called **neurotransmitters** also appear to be involved in anger control. Neurotransmitters are special chemicals the brain uses so that nerve cells can communicate with each other. Serotonin is one type of neurotransmitter. Low levels of serotonin have been linked with violent behavior. Medicines used to treat anxiety and depression help the serotonin in the brain to work harder. This may be why people who are depressed and angry find that these medicines often help both symptoms.

FIGHT, FLIGHT, OR FREEZE

Have you heard of the "fight, flight, or freeze" response? This is your body's natural reaction to danger. When we humans think we are in danger, our limbic system produces adrenaline. This speeds up our heart rate and breathing in order to get us ready to fight the danger, run away from the danger, or freeze—stay very still so that the danger passes us by.

Keep in mind that for most of human history, our survival has depended on our body's ability to sense danger and leap quickly into action. The danger we faced usually was an attacking creature or some other physical threat.

But most of today's threats are not physical. We are more likely to feel attacked by words than by a wild animal. Still, our bodies react with fight, flight, or freeze. We get revved up. Our hearts pound and our fists clench. We get ready for a physical fight. But with today's threats, logic or reason usually are more helpful.

Here's another way to think about it. Imagine your brain is a car. Normally, your frontal lobes drive and your reptilian brain (the limbic system) sits in the passenger seat. Now imagine you're driving down the road when you see something that triggers your anger. Sometimes your reptilian brain reaches over and grabs the steering wheel before your frontal lobes can do anything. Next thing you know, you're swerving out of control.

Of course, you probably don't lose control or get into a fight *every* time you get angry. That's because your frontal lobes help interpret situations. They can turn off the fight, flight, or freeze response. But as a teen you may have a harder time with this because your frontal lobes are not fully mature.

Again, it's important to remember that your fight, flight, or freeze response isn't an excuse for losing control. Many things affect your ability to control your anger, including things that have happened to you. But your anger is still your responsibility.

Brain Imaging

Imagine actually watching the brain in action! That's what psychiatrist Daniel Amen has found a way to do. **Brain imaging** is a way of taking scans, or "pictures," of working brains by measuring how much blood is flowing to different parts of the brain.

Dr. Amen has conducted brain scans on thousands of patients. Many of those patients had problems with aggression or anger. He has found that certain brain problems may be related to problems with aggression.

You can see these brain scans and find out more at Dr. Amen's Web site: www.brainplace.com/bp.

WHAT CAN YOU DO?

You can train your brain to turn off the fight, flight, or freeze reaction by training it to interpret things differently. If your brain stops seeing everything as so threatening, it can help you not overreact. The trick is learning how to think about situations differently so they don't seem so threatening.

One way to do that is to identify the early signs that you're getting angry—such as feeling your muscles tense up. (These are your **anger warning signs.** Maybe you wrote about them in your journal on page 19.) When this happens, take a deep breath and ask yourself two questions: Is this worth getting upset about? What's a better way of thinking about this situation so I won't feel so upset?

Thinking this way takes practice, just like learning a sport. But doing it can keep your brain from turning on the fight, flight, or freeze reaction. That makes it a lot easier to stay calmer even when you're angry.

To learn more, check out the Public Broadcasting Services Web site, "Inside the Teenage Brain." This site explains teen brain development and how it relates to teen behavior. You can watch a video describing how teenage brains develop.

www.pbs.org/wgbh/pages/frontline/shows/teenbrain

Another PBS Web site is "The Secret Life of the Brain." This site lets you look at the brain in 3-D.

www.pbs.org/wnet/brain/3d/index.html

3
THE TEENAGE RAGE GAUGE: GETTING TO KNOW YOUR ANGER

> I can control my anger by going in my room and drawing. —Boy, 14

> I don't control my anger. I start to cry and hit things. And my head hurts! —Girl, 16

> I hurt my brother—stabbed him in the leg. —Boy, 14

> When I'm mad I just want to be alone. And if anyone comes around they might get hit. —Boy, 17

> I feel very mad and sad. I try to find an escape by hanging out with my cousins. I feel the urge to drink and smoke. —Girl, 17

In chapters 1 and 2, you started thinking about what makes you mad. You thought about how you act and how it feels when you're mad. In this chapter, you can get an even better measure of your anger using a quiz called the Teenage Rage Gauge.

Photocopy the quiz on pages 26 and 27 and circle your answer for each statement. If you can't photocopy the quiz, write your answers in your journal or on a sheet of paper.

After you finish the quiz, take a closer look at your answers. For each statement you said was "Often True" or "Very Often True," think of an example from your life that demonstrates that statement. For example, maybe you circled "Often" for statement 3, "Little things bother me a lot." If so, think of an example of a little thing that bothers you a lot. Think about a time this happened. How did you react? Thinking about this will give you a better idea of how your anger problems are affecting your life.

Did your answers reveal any problems you might have in your relationships? For example, did you answer "Often True" or "Very Often True" for questions 6–9 or 20? You might get a lot of help from Part 3 of this book, Anger in Relationships.

Are there some statements on the quiz that bother you more than others? Put a checkmark next to those statements. These may be hot anger triggers for you. Try to avoid situations where those triggers may come up. If you can't avoid them, plan what you'll do or say. That way you won't get caught by surprise and react angrily.

The Teenage Rage Gauge

Respond to each statement by circling how often it is true for you.

1. I have trouble controlling my anger.   Never   Sometimes   Often   Very Often

2. I lose my temper easily.   Never   Sometimes   Often   Very Often

3. Little things bother me a lot.   Never   Sometimes   Often   Very Often

4. I yell or swear at others when I get angry.   Never   Sometimes   Often   Very Often

5. Anger gets me what I want from others.   Never   Sometimes   Often   Very Often

6. I say mean things when I'm angry that I later regret.   Never   Sometimes   Often   Very Often

7. If someone has hurt me, I have trouble letting go of it.   Never   Sometimes   Often   Very Often

8. I tease or make fun of others, even if it upsets them.   Never   Sometimes   Often   Very Often

9. It's hard for me to forgive others who have hurt me, even when they apologize.   Never   Sometimes   Often   Very Often

10. I get jealous of others.   Never   Sometimes   Often   Very Often

11. I think about getting revenge on people who have hurt me.   Never   Sometimes   Often   Very Often

12. I play violent video games or watch violent movies.   Never   Sometimes   Often   Very Often

13. If I'm angry at someone, I have trouble talking to them about it.   Never   Sometimes   Often   Very Often

14. I show my anger in little ways, such as by being late or "forgetting" to do things I promised to do (like chores or homework).   Never   Sometimes   Often   Very Often

15. I show my anger by doing a lousy job if I'm asked to do something I don't want to do.	Never	Sometimes	Often	Very Often
16. I am very impatient when driving (for example, I yell or swear if another car cuts in front of me).	Never	Sometimes	Often	Very Often
17. I get tense when others are angry.	Never	Sometimes	Often	Very Often
18. When I get angry, I feel out of control.	Never	Sometimes	Often	Very Often
19. I break the law when I'm angry.	Never	Sometimes	Often	Very Often
20. I have lost friends (or girlfriends or boyfriends) because of my anger.	Never	Sometimes	Often	Very Often
21. I throw things, slam doors, or break things when I'm angry.	Never	Sometimes	Often	Very Often
22. I hit, punch, push, or otherwise hurt others when I'm angry.	Never	Sometimes	Often	Very Often
23. I use drugs or alcohol to calm down when I'm upset.	Never	Sometimes	Often	Very Often

How many times did you answer "Often True" or "Very Often True"? There is no certain score that means you have an anger problem. But answers of "Often True" and "Very Often True" can help you learn about your struggles to control anger. This quiz helps you see how you handle anger and what you need to look out for. It can help you decide what anger issues you might want to work on first.

Take this quiz again every few weeks as you work on controlling your anger. See if the number of "Often True" or "Very Often True" answers changes as time goes by. This is a good way of tracking your progress.

Journal — Get a Gauge on Your Rage

Did you learn anything new after taking the teenage Rage Gauge quiz? Did any of your answers surprise you? Write, draw, or talk to someone about what it was like to look at your anger this way.

Next, think of three specific things about your life that will be better once you get a stronger handle on your anger. Put them in your journal. Think of these as goals to shoot for. Keep these goals in mind as you read the rest of this book. They can help motivate you during the challenging task of improving your anger control.

Now look at your answers again. Did you answer "Often True" or "Very Often True" to one or more of questions 19–23? If so, your anger already has become destructive. You may have damaged relationships or hurt yourself physically. You may have put your future at risk. But it's important to remember: **That's in the past.**

It can be disheartening to learn your anger is destructive. You may have to work harder than most people to control your anger. You may need professional help. But if it's important to you, and you're willing to work at it, you *can* do it. Check out Chapter 12 (How Treatment Can Help) for more information on getting professional help.

I got expelled from school for getting into too many fights, because people pick at me until I break. In the end, fighting is not worth it. It's just letting people know if they mess with you, you'll get mad. And even if you beat the crap out of them, they still win. —Girl, 15

Finally, ask a couple family members or friends to rate you on the Rage Gauge. Compare their answers about you to your own. If they give you more "Often True" and "Very Often True" answers than you gave yourself, you may not be fully aware of how serious your anger problems are. Talk to them about the differences in your ratings. Ask them to take the quiz for themselves, too. Ask them to talk about which statements are problems for them and what strategies they use to handle their anger.

Remember, it's not wrong—or bad or unhealthy—to be angry. Problems come from how you express, or show, your anger. So far in this book you've done a lot to figure out what your anger problem is like. In Part 2, you'll learn ways to control your anger. You'll also learn ideas for communicating your anger in healthy ways.

PART 2
TAME THE FLAMES

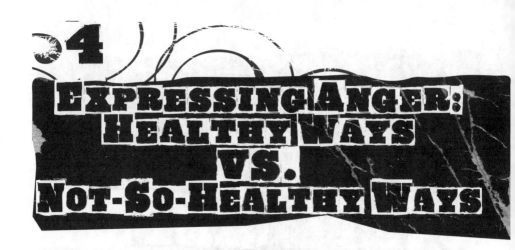

4

EXPRESSING ANGER:
HEALTHY WAYS
VS.
NOT-SO-HEALTHY WAYS

I'm in foster care, and it really makes me mad that I can't see my family more often. But what really gets me is when people spread rumors about me doing stuff with guys. I was about to fight this girl in my neighborhood for saying stuff about me, but I knew that if I did, it will be a lot longer before I get to go home. Instead, I talked to her about it. She apologized and now we're getting along. I was able to just let it go. What's also helped me with my anger is learning how to say how I feel when I'm mad. Instead of going off on my mom, I just tell her how her actions hurt me. She listens a lot better when I do it that way, though I'm not going to lie—it's still hard.—*Girl, 16*

I chew some gum and take a deep breath.—*Boy, 13*

I go someplace and pray. —Boy, 18

When I'm angry, I don't know whether to cry or just get really mad. But then I go play a game of basketball. —Girl, 16

I just listen to some music and get my mind off the person I am angry at. —Boy, 17

People express their anger in all sorts of ways. Some people lash out or explode. Others bury their anger inside. Many people yell at each other, and some resort to violence. When expressing anger, there are healthy ways and not-so-healthy ways. How can you tell the difference?

Healthy expressions of anger can make you feel better without hurting others or yourself. They may help build a solution to the problem. Unhealthy expressions of anger usually hurt other people or yourself—or both. While a healthy expression of anger can help fix a problem, an unhealthy one cannot. In fact, it can make problems worse. Expressing anger in an unhealthy way often makes you more angry. It can also trigger anger (or *more* anger) in the person you're mad at. That only adds fuel to the fire of anger.

This chapter helps you understand the differences between healthy and not-so-healthy ways of expressing anger. It also provides examples of both, to help you see which way you're expressing anger.

HEALTHY WAYS OF EXPRESSING ANGER

You may need to practice expressing your anger in healthy ways—ways that don't hurt anyone. Like anything you learn, it takes time to get it right. Here are some examples.

Use I-Messages

If you're mad at someone, talk to that person. Be assertive but not aggressive. That means stating your feelings or asking for what you want in a calm, respectful tone. Don't attack or use mean words. That way you're more likely to be understood.

One of the simplest and most effective strategies is to use an **I-message.** Say what you feel by saying the word "I" and then following it with a feeling. Then you can add what made you feel that way.

Here are a few examples:

- I feel angry when you take my things without asking.
- I feel frustrated when you don't let me go out with my friends.
- I feel sad when you call me names.

By starting with your own feelings, it's easier to avoid name-calling or saying other hurtful things.

You can expand the I-message to include why you feel the way you do and what you'd like the other person to do differently. Here's a model to use:

I feel _____ when you _____ because _____.

I'd like it if you _____.

Here are some examples:

- I feel annoyed when you make those clicking noises because I'm trying to watch TV. I'd like it if you would make them in another room.

- I feel upset when you talk to your ex-girlfriend because I'm scared that you might still have feelings for her. I'd like it if you'd let me know when you've talked to her, instead of keeping it a secret.

- I get really mad when you make jokes about my family because it's insulting. I'd like it if you'd stop, even if you are just kidding.

Talk to Someone You Trust

Sometimes you may be too angry to talk to the person who made you mad. Or maybe you can't talk to him or her for some reason. Maybe the person won't talk to you—or won't listen to you.

If you can't talk to the person you're mad at, talk to someone you trust. Let them know how you feel. Maybe he or she can give you some advice. Or maybe not. Either way, it's healing just to talk. Sometimes, talking can help you figure out why you're so mad. Or venting your feelings with someone you trust can help you feel less angry. That can make it easier to approach the person you're upset with in a more respectful and caring way.

Get Some Exercise

If you don't feel like talking to anyone, an easy way to vent your anger is by doing something physical. Let out your angry feelings by running, swimming, dancing, skating or skateboarding, playing basketball, lifting weights, doing karate, doing push-ups, taking swings in the batting cage, or whatever you like to do. You can even do physical chores like scrubbing the kitchen floor, sweeping, weeding, mowing, or beating the dust out of couch cushions.

Doing something physical gets your blood pumping and produces endorphins. Endorphins are chemicals in your body that make you feel good. It's hard to hold onto anger when you feel good. Exercising also gives you time to calm down and think about what you want to do or say. Maybe later you can try to talk to someone.

What ticks me off the most is trying to communicate something to my mom and getting her to understand—it's hard to break that communication barrier, especially over hot-button issues such as TV, homework, and computers. Even something as simple as not being able to take a shower in the morning because my mom's in the shower can set me up for a bad day—then my anger just builds and builds until it explodes. What helps me deal with my anger are two things. First, getting outside and into nature helps a lot. The warmer weather and being able to ride my bike helps relieve stress. Second, I'm now able to actually talk with my mom about issues. If we can talk and get it out, it helps me get over my anger a lot better. It also helps when my mom lets me know that I'm crossing the line and "getting pissy" with her—I back down instead of making it worse by yelling.—**Boy, 16**

Put It in Writing

Write down your feelings. This helps many people feel better, because they feel like they've gotten the anger *out* of them by writing about it. You can write in your journal or write a letter to the person you're mad at. When you write your feelings in a letter, even if you never plan to send it, it helps you sort out your feelings and calm down.

I write poems when I'm mad. —*Girl, 14*

I will talk to someone, or write down my feelings. —*Boy, 13*

Important: Be careful *not* to express your feelings using instant messaging, text messaging, or email. It can be hard for others to understand how you're trying to come across. They may think you're attacking them even when you're not.

Do Something Positive with Your Anger

If you're angry about an injustice, such as poverty, prejudice, or a political issue, put your anger to good use. You can do something about injustice. Write a letter to the editor of your local paper or write an article for your school newspaper. You can volunteer for a cause or start a school club so other students can join you in fighting for your cause. Call, email, or write to your government representatives.

When a guy hits or abuses a girl, I get mad and I have to do something. —*Boy, 15*

What makes me mad is all the things that go on in the world that people know are wrong, but they do nothing. —*Girl, 15*

Things that make me mad:

- People who complain but never want to work toward changing the situation.
- The unequal treatment among different cultures and ethnic groups.
- Society and its "guidelines"—how you should look, dress, etc.
- Being unable to help people who have incurable illnesses.

—Girl, 16

You can also do something positive with more personal anger. Anger can give you energy and focus. If you're mad because you had a fight with a friend at school, put that energy into a project. Build a skateboard ramp or practice your karate. If you're mad at your brother for taking your phone, fix a broken bike.

Journal — Healthy Ways of Expressing Anger

Write about one or more healthy ways you have expressed your anger. How did it work for you? Which of these ideas do you want to try in the future? Why? Can you think of a situation that you didn't handle very well that might have gone better if you had used one of these strategies?

NOT-SO-HEALTHY WAYS TO EXPRESS YOUR ANGER

When your anger causes trouble or pain for you or someone else, you may be expressing it in an unhealthy way. Ask yourself if you're being respectful of yourself or the person you're mad at. Or think of how you'd react if someone treated you the way you're treating them.

Here are some unhealthy ways people commonly express their anger. Do any of these sound like something you do?

Being Violent

Violence is when someone uses physical force to hurt someone or something. It means being destructive. Examples of violence include:

- Hitting or otherwise hurting people (including yourself)
- Damaging property (such as punching a hole in the wall)
- Breaking things, especially things that are important to someone else

When I get mad I punch things. I broke my hand in anger.—Boy, 16

I punch stuff, or get a knife and stab the wall.—Girl, 14

I beat the crap out of this kid for talking about my grandmother, and his parents pressed charges.—Boy, 14

Many people resort to violence when they're angry. It can sometimes feel good at first to vent this way. But violence usually leads to someone being hurt, one way or another.

If the adrenaline of anger leads you to feel violent, exercise can help. It can burn off the extra energy and make you feel better. If you react to anger with violence most of the time, get help. Talk to an adult you trust. You may need to get help from a counselor or therapist. Read Chapter 12 to learn more.

Swearing and Saying Mean Things

It's important to pay attention to the words you choose when angry. Think of all the mean words you use when you argue with someone. These include all of the curse words and insults. Those words can hurt. And you can't take them back once you've said them.

Hurtful words also tend to add fuel to the fire of anger. People often get more angry when they say or hear hurtful words. Use respectful and calming words instead. Try not to blame the other person, even if you think he or she is at fault. It's hard to do when you're angry, but try to stay calm. If you really want to be respected, you have to be respectful.

A good way to make your point respectfully is to use I-messages. Go to pages 34–35 to refresh your memory on how to do that.

Like violence, cussing out someone can make you feel good at first. Curse words are some of the angriest words we have. And they cause hurt when you use them in anger. If you need to use them, say them where nobody can hear you.

Stuffing Anger

Some people think it's bad to express anger in any way. They may have been taught that showing anger is immature. Or maybe they've seen people express anger in violent ways, and they think that's what anger is. So instead of expressing anger directly, they keep it all inside. Or else they do things to direct their anger at themselves. They may not even realize they're doing this.

If you don't let out your anger, you create tension inside yourself. This can cause headaches, stomachaches, or muscle soreness. Stuffing can lead to other problems, too. Some people get depressed or down on themselves. They think it's their fault that they're angry. They think they're a bad person for feeling that way. Some people use alcohol or drugs to take away the tension caused by anger. Others injure themselves intentionally by hitting themselves, banging their head, or cutting themselves. Creating physical pain can distract them from their emotional pain.

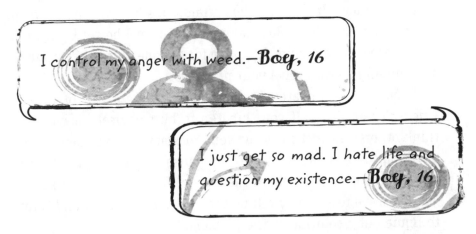

I control my anger with weed.—Boy, 16

I just get so mad. I hate life and question my existence.—Boy, 16

All of these ways of dealing with anger are unhealthy. It's best not to hurt others with your anger, of course. But stuffing anger hurts you.

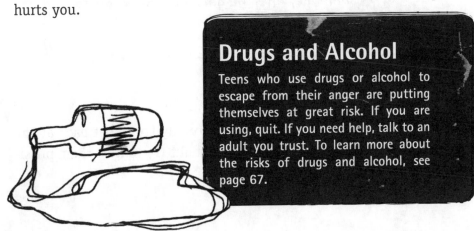

Drugs and Alcohol

Teens who use drugs or alcohol to escape from their anger are putting themselves at great risk. If you are using, quit. If you need help, talk to an adult you trust. To learn more about the risks of drugs and alcohol, see page 67.

Being Passive-Aggressive

You read about being passive-aggressive on page 16. That's when people show their anger indirectly, so they don't have to admit they're mad. They might "forget" to do things they said they'd do. Or they might do things that indirectly hurt the person they're mad at. That way they don't have to admit they hurt that person on purpose. Being passive-aggressive *does* hurt—both you and the other person. It is an unhealthy way of expressing anger.

Making Threats

Threatening others, even if you don't intend to follow through, is cruel and unfair. It makes others afraid. This behavior might help you feel better at first. But making yourself feel better by scaring someone else is bullying. It's hard for anyone to respect a bully, and bullying doesn't solve your problems.

Some people threaten to hurt themselves instead of others. This isn't fair either. If you threaten to hurt yourself, maybe you think others will feel sorry for you. You may believe they will do anything to keep you from hurting yourself. But forcing others to be nice to you usually makes them resentful. You're more likely to get a positive reaction by telling them why you're upset and trying to figure out a solution to the problem.

I know someone, when he gets mad, he wants to kill himself.—Boy, 16

Getting Revenge

Some people, when they're angry, naturally try to get back at the person who made them angry. They might try to hurt them physically or emotionally.

It might seem like getting revenge will make you feel better. But usually it doesn't. Instead, it turns anger into a cycle. After one person gets revenge, then the other person will probably want revenge. It could go on and on. Revenge doesn't solve any problems, and will almost certainly make them worse.

Journal When Anger Hurts Someone

Write about a time you hurt someone—physically or emotionally—with your anger. What happened? How did you feel afterward? Do you still have a relationship with the person you hurt? How has it changed?

Now write about a time someone hurt *you* with their anger. How has your relationship with that person changed? Does remembering how you felt give you more motivation to control your anger? Why or why not?

If you don't want to write, draw a picture or talk to someone about these ideas.

When people get angry, they have two choices. One choice is to react in a way that will hurt someone—to add fuel to the fire, so it blazes higher or explodes. The other choice is to catch it early and keep it from raging. Your anger is real and you deserve to let it burn itself out. But don't fuel it by being hurtful to others or yourself.

Expressing anger without hurting is healthy, but it's not always easy. The next chapter has "firewalls"—tools to help you do this.

5

FIREWALLS: TOOLS FOR CONTROLLING ANGER

Sometimes when I'm mad, I feel helpless. Sometimes I think of running away. I yell, and then after I calm down I feel sad and angry at myself for yelling at my loved ones. My advice to other teens is, when there's an argument, go for a walk and when you get back the argument will be over and you'll find all that exercise and fresh air will do you a world of good.—Boy, 16

I don't talk to the person who made me mad. I just get away.—Boy, 15

Try to take your mind off of the issue. Talk to someone if you need help. Also, don't let anger bottle up because that anger is going to burst one day and there may be consequences for it.—Girl, 17

I *hate* being angry, it sucks. I feel tense and have a lot of bottled-up energy. I try to go somewhere to be alone where no one can bug me. Sometimes I exercise, which usually works the best.—*Girl, 15*

When I'm mad, I go do something like play soccer or ride my bike.—*Girl, 16*

My muscles get all tight when I'm angry. I punch my punching bag, and that helps. If you're mad, get a punching bag.—*Boy, 14*

After reading Chapter 4, you know the difference between healthy and not-so-healthy ways of expressing anger. But just knowing the difference doesn't make it easy to do what's best. It's usually easier to yell, scream, or throw or break things when you're angry. Or it might seem natural to stuff your anger, or to be passive-aggressive.

Fortunately, you can help yourself by using the firewalls in this chapter. Firewalls are tools to help you control your anger by choosing healthy reactions to it. Some firewalls you use when you're *not* mad. These will help you prevent anger flare-ups and be better prepared for them when they do come. Some firewalls you use when you *are* mad. These will help you stay in control when you're feeling ticked off. The more you practice these tips, the easier it gets to keep the fire safe.

FIREWALLS FOR BEFORE YOU GET MAD

The easiest and most effective way to keep anger under control is to plan ahead. You can do things to try to prevent anger. Another part of planning ahead is preparing what you'll do when anger comes. After all, you can't always prevent it.

The firewalls you're about to read involve preventing and preparing for anger. Even if you don't have as much trouble turning off your anger as others, it's still smart to plan ahead.

Know and Use Your Warning Signs

If you've been using a journal, you've already started thinking about your anger warning signs. Anger warning signs are ways to tell if your anger is getting out of control. The signs are usually **physical, behavioral,** or **emotional.**

Physical signs are what your body is telling you. These can include feeling tense, your face turning red, getting hot or sweating, feeling your heart beat faster, noticing your arms or legs shaking, or feeling a surge of energy.

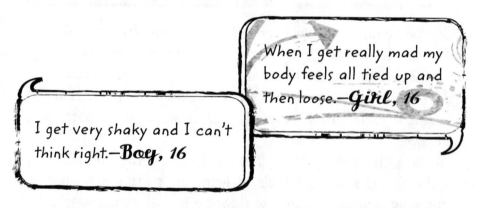

When I get really mad my body feels all tied up and then loose.—*Girl, 16*

I get very shaky and I can't think right.—*Boy, 16*

Behavioral signs are things you say or do. Sometimes, you don't realize you're angry until you say or do something. Examples include raising your voice or yelling, hitting others, throwing things, pacing back and forth, clenching your fists, or banging your fists on a table or against a wall or door.

One of my friends got in trouble with the school because he hit someone in the face and broke his nose.—**Boy, 16**

In school this girl kept making fun of me and I finally called her a b****. She pushed me and I did it back and we got into a fight.—*Girl, 16*

Emotional signs are the feelings you have. You may feel anger exploding inside you, or you may feel humiliated, dissed, attacked, or even afraid. Sometimes being afraid that something bad will happen can trigger anger.

Anger can sneak up on you quickly. It's hard to think about the consequences of your actions when you're mad. If you are aware of your warning signs, you can plan how to react when you notice them. Then you can take action before your anger gets out of control.

Predict Anger Situations

Sometimes anger surprises you. But often, you can tell ahead of time what situations are a risk for anger. If you identify these situations, you can avoid them or make a plan to deal with them.

For example, imagine you and your mom are about to talk about weekend plans. You think your mom will give you a hard time about your plans, and you might end up yelling. To avoid that, talk with her ahead of time. Let her know you're worried you might argue, and you're going to do your best to stay calm. Also let her know that if you start to get upset you're going to make a time-out signal with your hands. This is a signal to her that your anger is starting to get the best of you and you need to take a break. After you signal time out, go for a walk before continuing the discussion.

Here's another example. Imagine your boyfriend or girlfriend just dumped you for your good friend. Now, imagine there's a party this weekend, and you know they'll both be there. There's a good chance that if you see them together you might get pretty mad. You don't know how you'll react if you get that mad. The best plan here might be to avoid that situation entirely by skipping the party.

He Who Holds the Cowboy Hat Talks

Another plan if you think you might argue with someone is to take turns talking. Some therapists suggest you use a prop. If you're holding the prop, you get to talk. If someone else is holding the prop, that person gets to talk. Everyone who isn't holding the prop listens quietly. Picking something funny such as a banana, a goofy hat, or a stuffed animal can help break the tension. Humor is always a great remedy for anger!

Try to avoid conflicts between yourself and other people. —*Girl, 16*

Choose Good Times to Resolve Conflicts

Find the right time to talk about issues that might make people angry. It's usually not a good idea to jump into a touchy subject right after school or work when everyone's tired. It's also best to avoid times when you or the other person is busy, like before school when everyone's getting ready to go. When you're tired or busy, you're much more likely to lose control.

A better approach to talking about tense subjects is to agree ahead of time when to talk about them. Plan this out with your mom or dad or whoever you're going to talk with. That way, you'll both be prepared to talk about problems at a time that works for everyone. If possible, pick a specific day and time to talk. You can even put it on the family calendar or post a note on the refrigerator to remind everyone.

Take a Break from Anger

Make a promise to yourself not to act on angry feelings, no matter what. Not forever, just for 24 hours. That means no yelling, hitting, swearing, cursing, or throwing or banging things. This gives you a chance to see how else you can react to anger triggers. Also, it shows you that you *can* stay calm.

If you think it would help, share your promise with others you care about. If others know about it, it's harder for you to break your agreement. Ask them to let you know if they see you starting to show anger.

It may help you to sign a contract. This makes the agreement feel more important so you're less likely to break it. Your contract can look something like the form on page 50. You can photocopy this contract, if you like, or create your own version.

Anger Control Contract

DATE _____ TIME_____

I, _____,
(your name)

PROMISE THAT FOR THE NEXT 24 HOURS I WILL NOT LET MYSELF SHOW ANGER. I WILL STAY CALM NO MATTER WHAT HAPPENS. IF MY FRIENDS AND/OR FAMILY NOTICE ME SHOWING ANGER, I GIVE THEM PERMISSION TO LET ME KNOW.

_____
Your signature

_____
Signature of friend or family member

Find an Anger Partner

Because learning to control your anger can be so hard, sometimes you need help. One way to get help is to have an anger partner. An anger partner is a friend or relative you can call when you are afraid you're going to act out on your anger. Ask someone you trust if you can call him or her when you feel anger taking over. That person can help you calm down and remind you of good coping strategies to use.

Important!

If you're so mad you think you might seriously injure someone, talk to an adult right away. Ask him or her to help you keep from doing something you'll regret. If you have a counselor, see if you can reach your counselor for advice. Most counselors have an emergency number you can call. It's better to get help than to harm someone and end up in jail. See Chapter 12 for more on counseling.

I think the best thing to do is find someone who really loves you that you can love, too, and talk to him or her whenever you're mad or hurt. —*Girl, 15*

Journal Identify Anger Partners

Write down the names of people you think would be willing to be your anger partner. then ask each of them if they're willing to help. For the people who agree, write down the best ways to get a hold of them (a phone number and email address, for example) and when it's okay to contact them. You might also want to keep a copy of this list in your wallet or purse in case you're away from home when you need it.

FIREWALLS FOR WHEN YOU ARE MAD

Hey, you're going to get mad—even if you do your best to avoid it. When you do, the following firewalls can help you keep cool.

You'll probably want to try them all and see which ones work best for you. Some teens like to write about them in their journals. They keep track of how it goes when they use each firewall. You can also write each one out on a colored index card to help you remember them. Carry the cards with you, and when you find yourself getting angry, review the cards for ideas on what to do. You can even make notes on your cell phone if you have one. Or just write them down on a scrap of paper and carry it in your wallet.

Count to Ten

This is an old strategy that works well. Counting buys you time to cool down. The longer you count, the more time your anger has to cool. And the easier it will be for the thinking part of your brain to kick in and gain control.

When you count, be sure to do it slowly. Say, "One one-thousand, two one-thousand, three one-thousand," and so on. If you need to, count higher—it might take until you reach 100 before you've calmed down!

Leave the Situation

If your anger is increasing quickly and you're not sure you can control it, get away from the situation if you can. The longer you stick around, the more likely you'll do something you'll regret. It's far better to walk away if you're angry with people than to throw something at them or cuss them out. If you can, let them know what you're doing and why. This can help at school, too. Some examples are:

- "Mom, I'm about to blow. I need to get away for a bit—I'll be back when I'm calmer."
- "Mrs. Jones, I need a break. Can I get a drink of water?"
- "I've got to get out of here before I do something stupid."
- "I'm too ticked to talk about this now. Let me cool down and we'll talk tomorrow, okay?"

Some teens prefer to be alone when they're angry, even after that first flare-up fades away. If you're still feeling ticked, it's okay to stay by yourself for a while. Then you don't have to worry about keeping your anger under control or saying the wrong thing. You're giving yourself a break. In a way, it's like taking a pot of boiling water off the stove. It slowly cools down until it's safer to handle. After a while, the anger starts to fade and you may be ready to try some of the healthy ways of expressing your anger.

I just want to be left alone when I'm mad. I go into my room and lie in my bed in the dark. —Girl, 16

I walk away and find somewhere to cool off and think things over. —Boy, 16

Yell into a Pillow

This may sound a bit silly. Some people feel a lot better when they scream or yell, but they don't want to hurt the feelings (or the ears) of those around them. Screaming into a pillow can let out some of the anger. Then you can talk later about what's bothering you.

Warning!

For some people, expressing their anger this way can actually fuel the fire. If you notice your anger getting more intense when you yell into your pillow, try a different strategy.

Get Moving

Go for a walk, run down the street, work out at a gym, do sit-ups and push-ups in your living room, do jumping jacks, shoot some hoops, ride a bike, turn on music and dance like crazy, or lift dumbbells. There are hundreds of ways to get exercise. All kinds of exercise release endorphins, chemicals that make you feel better and help you calm down.

Exercise also helps use up the adrenaline that pumps through your system when your fight, flight, or freeze response gets triggered. (Remember fight, flight, or freeze, from Chapter 2? That's when your brain thinks a threat is a physical danger. See pages 21–22.) In a way, exercising tricks your body into thinking that the "danger" has passed. That's because moving quickly is one of the strategies ancient humans used to protect themselves from dangerous animals or other tribes. Once your brain thinks the danger has passed, it signals your body to slow down and return to normal.

Playing sports can also be a good way to take out your anger in a more acceptable way. Anger on the playing field can help you perform better in competitive events. The adrenaline of anger can give you better focus and more energy. Of course, you have to be sure not to break the rules as a result of your anger.

Do a sport that allows you to use that anger.—**Boy**, *15*

I usually kick my soccer ball around. That helps with the anger.—**Girl**, *15*

Hit a Punching Bag

Some people's anger is so strong they can't seem to calm down without hitting something. This can lead to many broken doors and damaged walls that can be expensive to repair. It can also lead to people getting hurt. By hitting a punching bag, pillow, or mattress, you have a physical release without destroying anything or hurting anyone. Many sporting goods stores carry punching bags.

Warning!

Scientists have found that hitting a punching bag when you're angry can make *some* people angrier, instead of calmer. It can keep the adrenaline rush going, which keeps the emotional part of your brain overstimulated. If you find that hitting makes things worse, pick another strategy to use.

Chill out. Hit a pillow or something soft, then when you are cooled down, talk about it with someone.—**Boy**, *15*

I usually scream into a pillow, punch a pillow, or go for a run. After I do that and have time to think about what happened, I am calmed down.—**Girl**, *15*

Take Deep Breaths

Most people don't think about their breathing very much. But taking deep breaths helps you relax. When you're stressed or panicked—for example, when you're mad—your breathing usually gets quick and shallow. Breathing like that adds to your stress. Deep breathing can reverse this process and help your body slow down.

Start by placing your hand on the lower part of your stomach. Breathe in slowly, counting slowly to five. (One one-thousand, two one-thousand, three one-thousand, etc.) Try to fill up the bottom third of your lungs first, followed by the middle third, and then the top third. Feel your stomach rise as you fill up your lungs. Once your lungs are full, reverse the process. Empty your lungs, counting to five as you do. Start from the top and work your way down. Imagine the angry feelings leaving your body as you blow out. Picture your anger as red smoke rising harmlessly into the sky.

Think Fire-Extinguishing Thoughts

Things that happen don't make you mad by themselves. What you *think* about those things makes a difference. For example, let's say your mom asks you to clean your room and you get really mad. You end up screaming and calling her names. You didn't get ticked off *just because* she asked you to clean your room. It may be a perfectly reasonable request. Maybe you've done it before without blowing up. So why did you get so upset this time? The difference is your attitude about her request. How you feel about it makes the difference between blowing up or just doing it.

Well-known therapist Albert Ellis developed a theory called ABC. The ABC theory explains how people's thoughts about a situation determine how they react. Here's how it works:

A = Activating event. This is what *happened* that triggered your angry feelings. In this case, it was your mom telling you to clean your room.

B = Beliefs, thoughts, or attitude you have about the event. In our example, it could have been that you thought your mom was getting on your case and being unfair. Or maybe you thought she was trying to upset you on purpose.

C = Consequences, or feelings, that result from the **Activating event** *combined with* your **Beliefs** or attitude about the event. The consequences might be that you feel upset, angry, sad, anxious, or many other feelings. In the room-cleaning example, the consequences were that you got really mad.

When you look at anger this way, you can see a way to calm yourself after anger strikes. When you get mad, look hard at your beliefs about the trigger that made you mad. Do these thoughts make sense? Can you change them? When you feel anger flaring up, ask yourself: "Why am I getting so angry about this? Why am I reacting so strongly? Is my level of anger justified?"

Going back to the room-cleaning example, here are some possible beliefs or attitudes that could be fueling anger about cleaning your room:

- She yelled at me when she told me to clean my room— that's disrespectful.

- She knows I just got home from school. Why can't she let me relax?

- She always bosses me around. Maybe if she'd ask nicely I'd be more willing to do it.

- How come she doesn't bug my brothers or sisters about their rooms? Their rooms are worse than mine.

- It's my room—she has no right to make me clean it. I'll do it if I want to.

All these beliefs or attitudes are going to fuel your anger. They are ways of throwing gasoline on the fire, leading to explosions of anger. They can turn what may be a reasonable request into a bad situation.

Now compare those anger-producing beliefs with the following beliefs:

- She did ask me twice already to do it. She'll get off my back quicker if I just do it.

- She doesn't ask me that often—I guess I can do it.

- My mom does a lot for me—I guess I can make her happy by doing it.

- Maybe when I'm on my own I can keep my room a mess, but as long as I'm living in my mom's home, I'll have to follow her rules.

- It won't take me that long—then I can go out with my friends.

- Is it really that big of a deal? Is it worth getting into an argument over?

These are all extinguishing thoughts. They help you calm down, like using a fire extinguisher to put out a fire. It's a lot safer than pouring gasoline on the fire!

One way to come up with extinguishing thoughts is to identify your fire-producing thoughts first. Then turn those thoughts around. For example, if you think, "It's unfair!" try thinking, "Life isn't always fair—is that really so bad?" Another way is to ask other people to tell you what extinguishing thoughts they use. Write them down so you can practice using them when you need them.

It's not easy to change your thoughts about events. It takes courage to admit that your first thoughts might have been wrong. One way to practice doing this is to look back at times you were mad in the past. Look through your journal where you wrote about things that made you mad. See if you can identify the beliefs you had about those anger triggers. Looking back, were those beliefs right? What are some extinguishing thoughts you could have had instead?

Use Visualization

Your mind is a powerful tool. You can use it to help calm yourself by picturing positive images. Many famous athletes use visualization to psyche themselves up for a game or match with good success. Salespeople use it to help them sell their products. It can even help reduce stress and headaches, and lower your blood pressure.

Killing ANTs

Many negative beliefs have words like "always" or "never" in them. Dr. Daniel Amen calls these angry thoughts "ANTs—Automatic Negative Thoughts." They happen automatically—without thinking—and usually make you angrier. Here are some examples:

- "You *never* listen to me!"
- "I *never* get my way."
- "You're *always* late."

Dr. Amen recommends "killing the ANTs" by talking back to them with more accurate thoughts. For example, it's probably not true that your dad *never* listens to you. It's probably not true that your friend is *always* late. When you hear thoughts in your mind that have the words "always" or "never" in them, that's a good sign that you probably need to kill the ANTs. Look again at those negative beliefs and see if you can replace them with something that is more accurate and positive.

Visualization involves picturing things in your mind that you find calming. Some people imagine being on a beach, relaxing in a hammock, or playing a sport or game they love. Some people like to imagine themselves as one of their favorite role models from TV, movies, music, or sports. You can even imagine yourself as a superhero, if you're into comics, or a video game character.

To start using visualization, find a quiet place where you won't be interrupted. Take a couple deep breaths to help relax and clear your mind (see page 56). You can also play relaxing music if you like. Next, think of a person, place, or situation that is soothing to you or makes you feel happy and stress-free. Examples might include someone you care about, a place you've visited or would like to visit (such as the beach or next to a waterfall), or a situation such as winning a game and being cheered by your friends and family.

Now imagine you are in the scene you've chosen. Try to picture it in your mind as if you're watching a movie. You're the director. Imagine the scene unfolding, and focus on the sights, sounds, and smells of the scene. It's important to imagine lots of details. This gets your brain fully involved and makes it feel more real. Don't worry if other thoughts or images pop into your head. Gently direct yourself back to your image. Or go with the flow, as long as the images are positive and relaxing.

You can also use humor. Visualize something funny. For example, imagine the person you're angry at wearing a clown suit, being dipped in chocolate, or dressed in baby clothes. Imagine anything that you find funny and might bring a smile to your face.

Thought Stopping

This is a common technique for stopping all sorts of unwanted thoughts. All you have to do is say "Stop!" when angry thoughts come into your head. You can say it aloud or silently. If you're alone, yelling aloud can help take the energy out of your anger. Try this before your angry thoughts get too carried away. It may also help to switch gears and think about something else—something that calms you or makes you laugh.

***

Remember that getting control of your anger takes hard work and practice. By trying out the different tools in this chapter, you'll learn which ones work best for you.

6 LIFESTYLE CHOICES TO HELP YOU KEEP COOL

I get angry a lot. Little things pile up so much that I can't control it anymore. Then I get overwhelmed when people hit me with random stuff. When I get really mad, I don't feel like eating and sometimes won't eat for two days. I want to throw things but I don't. I curse a lot—I should stop that, especially since it got me in trouble when I cursed at my teacher. She yelled at me first for not being in the right seat in class and actually cussed at me first. I told her to leave me the f*** alone. I think she deserved it. Actually, I think the cursing is making me more mad. I once tried not cursing for a whole week and I was a lot happier.—**Boy, 14**

Try not to let little things get to you.—**Boy, 13**

Just try to stay positive. If you have a problem, talk about it to someone.—**Girl, 14**

It doesn't matter what they do or say, it's how you answer that matters.—**Boy, 18**

So far you've learned a lot about expressing and controlling anger. But you can also make healthier lifestyle choices. These choices will help you feel less anger—and less intense anger—in general. "Lifestyle" means the things you do every day, like eating, sleeping, going to school, hanging out with friends, and doing hobbies.

You might not think much about your lifestyle. It seems so automatic, you might not think it connects to your anger. But your lifestyle affects every minute of your life. The choices you make can have a big impact on how you feel. Many lifestyle choices can add to your stress, which makes you get angry easier. Healthier lifestyle choices can reduce your stress—making anger less of a problem.

EAT HEALTHY FOOD

You probably know that your body needs good food to work properly. But did you know healthy food is especially important for your brain? Your brain needs plenty of protein, vitamins, and minerals to help its different parts communicate with each other.

Brain Food

Your brain has important chemicals called neurotransmitters that are made of **protein.** If you don't get enough protein, your body won't have what it needs to work its best. **Vitamins** keep your brain cells healthy, so you can think clearly. They also help improve your mood. **Minerals** supply the energy your brain uses to communicate between its parts.

Foods with lots of protein include cheese, milk, meat (including fish), beans, eggs, nuts, soy, and tofu. Good sources of vitamins include colorful fruits and vegetables, like apples, oranges, bananas, broccoli, spinach, and tomatoes, as well as yogurt, tofu, and enriched breakfast cereals. Green vegetables are especially rich in important vitamins. You can find lots of minerals in vegetables like squash, tomatoes, and spinach, as well as in fruits, nuts, meat, and enriched grains. Generally, the darker a food's color, the healthier it is for you.

Eat something from each of these groups with every meal and drink plenty of water. Water keeps your brain hydrated, so it can function efficiently.

It's also a good idea to make sure you get enough healthy fats and oils in your diet. Fats found in foods such as fish, olive oil and other vegetable oils, nuts (such as almonds and walnuts), and seeds (such as pumpkin and sunflower seeds) are important for your body and brain to develop properly.

Fatty Acids, Nerve Cells, and Anger Control

Our brains consist of millions of nerve cells that communicate with each other through electrical impulses. Nerve cells have a membrane, or coating, called the myelin sheath, which is composed of fatty acids. These fatty acids are called essential fatty acids because our bodies can't make them. We must get them from our diet.

Some scientific studies have found that people who have problems with their mood may not have enough of these fatty acids. One type in particular, omega-3 fatty acids, are often low in people with mood or anger problems.

You can get plenty of omega-3 fatty acids from fish such as salmon and tuna or from walnuts or Brazil nuts. You can also take an omega-3 fatty acid supplement. (Be sure to check with your mom or dad and doctor first.) An added benefit is that it keeps your heart healthy, too!

Plan Regular Meals

One more thing: try not to go too long without eating. Many people get crabby when they don't eat regularly. This may be caused by a drop in blood sugar. Your body and your brain get their energy by breaking down food you eat. If you haven't eaten enough food lately, your body says "Feed me!" by making you grumpy.

If you tend to get grumpy or angry when you don't eat, keep a cereal bar or banana with you for when you get hungry. And try to eat at regular intervals. Many health and diet experts think eating smaller, more frequent meals during the day is better than eating three big meals. This keeps your energy level more even all day.

Of course, eating more frequently during the day is not an excuse to eat sugary snacks, like sodas, candy, or cookies. Sugary foods like this do give you a quick burst of energy, but your body processes it very quickly. That leaves you without enough energy to function. Another word about sodas and candy: foods like these, which are processed and packaged, usually have a lot of chemicals in them. These chemicals include dyes (to color the food) and preservatives (to help it stay fresh longer). They can make it harder for your brain to work well.

GET ENOUGH SLEEP

Like most things you do, controlling your anger takes energy. How do you get energy? One of the main ways is by eating healthy food. The other is by sleeping. Sleep recharges your body. You need lots of it to feel your best. When you don't get enough, you're more likely to be grouchy. You may be more easily set off, even by things that normally don't bother you.

Most teens need about nine hours of sleep a night. But many teens don't get that much. One reason is their circadian rhythm (the body's daily cycles of sleep and wake time). The natural circadian rhythm of teens tells them to fall asleep later and wake up later. Often, teens are up late talking on the phone, surfing the net, or IM-ing or texting their friends. To make things worse, school starts especially early for many high schoolers. If you have trouble falling asleep at night—or if you're just staying up—you will find that you're tired much of the time. You'll also have trouble concentrating in school.

Here are a few things you can do to get more sleep:

- Go to bed earlier—even just 30 minutes earlier at first. Every bit makes a difference.

- Avoid caffeinated drinks such as soda at night. Caffeine keeps you alert, so it's harder to sleep.

- Avoid stimulating activities such as video games before bed. They can make it hard to settle down for sleep.

- Get exercise—but not right before bed. Exercise can tire out your body, which is good for sleep. But it also increases your energy for a while right afterward.

- Have something small to eat, such as a bowl of cereal and milk, before bed. Milk is an especially good choice. It contains an amino acid called tryptophan that can make you sleepy. Caffeine-free herbal tea is another good choice.

LIMIT VIOLENT VIDEO GAMES AND TV SHOWS

Did you know that playing violent video games might make you more aggressive? That's what a 2000 study by two researchers found. The study showed that people who play violent video games are more likely to show aggressive behavior later on. Violent video games provide players with an opportunity to learn and practice aggressive responses to problem situations. Many video games allow users to attack realistic-looking humans in the game. It's possible that the adrenaline rush you get when playing (which is not discharged through exercise) can fuel your anger outbursts.

Watching violent TV shows or movies can make people more aggressive, too. Some people replay in their heads the violent scenes they watch. Then, when a frustrating situation comes along, they're more likely to respond aggressively. Also, the more you watch violent images, the less they bother you. Using aggression to deal with problems starts feeling more acceptable. And you may become less sensitive to the suffering of others.

But more research is needed on this topic. For example, it's possible that aggressive people are more drawn to these games and shows (rather than the games and shows make people aggressive). And for some, playing aggressive video games may actually help them vent their anger so they feel calmer afterward. Still, if you have problems with anger, you may be better off avoiding or at least limiting your violent video game playing and TV watching.

Playing violent video games helps me vent my anger. I know some people get more violent by playing them, but for me, it really depends on the video game. If I'm good at it and can nail the bad guys in the game, I feel better after. If I'm not so good at the game and I end up losing, my anger would get worse and that's when I'd take it out on the people around me, including my family.—Bay, 18

STAY AWAY FROM DRUGS AND ALCOHOL

Some teenagers turn to alcohol or other drugs to feel better or relieve stress. Being under the influence temporarily might take the edge off your anger or make you feel better about your problems. Drugs might seem exciting. But turning to illegal drugs or alcohol is very risky. They can cause damage to your body and brain. And it's easy to become addicted, especially for a teenager because your brain is not fully developed.

Certain drugs can make your anger worse. For example, alcohol is a depressant and relaxes the part of your brain that controls your impulses. If you're already angry, using alcohol or other depressants can bring out the worst in you. Many violent crimes are committed by people under the influence of alcohol or other drugs.

If you use alcohol or drugs to relieve stress or deal with problems, it's very important that you get help before your use causes even more problems. Talk to an adult you trust. You can also call the U.S. Department of Health to get information and help. Their Alcohol and Drug Information hotline is 1-800-729-6686. Your school guidance counselor also may know of resources in your area. Some schools even have support groups that meet in school.

ACCEPT LIFE ON LIFE'S TERMS

Let's face it: stuff happens that isn't fair, isn't right, and makes life more difficult. Sometimes anger comes from expecting that life *should* be fair. You might think:

- Everyone should get what they deserve.
- People should always be understanding.
- Things should always go according to plan.

But that's not how life is. People will tick you off, good luck doesn't always even out, and drivers will cut you off in traffic.

You're going to lose something important to you. People will break up with you. And your parents are not going to say "yes" to everything you ask.

But that doesn't mean you have to react with anger.

Remembering that life isn't always fair can help you not take things so personally. Ask yourself, "What's the worst that can happen?" When you do that, it's easier to see that most things that happen aren't *that* bad. So someone cuts you off or butts in front of you in line. You might be 30 seconds later. Big deal.

How about a bigger example? Say your boyfriend or girlfriend cheats on you or dumps you. What's the worst that can happen? You may be heartbroken for a while, but you will heal. Many relationships you have in high school won't last. That's hard to deal with. It hurts. But it's true.

Learning these things, and learning that life isn't fair, is part of growing up. It's a difficult part, but an important one. Some people will get better breaks than you. Some people will have it worse.

WRITE ABOUT YOUR FEELINGS

Your journal doesn't have to be just about anger. It's helpful to write, draw, or talk about all your feelings. Use your journal to get negative feelings out every day, before they build up. Journaling also helps you figure out why certain things are bothering you. It can even be a form of brainstorming. Use your journal to come up with ideas for how to handle anger situations. By thinking about them ahead of time, you are more likely to deal with them constructively. That way you avoid overreacting, and you get the respect you want.

But journaling isn't just for negative feelings. It's also a way of reminding yourself about the positive things that happen in your life. For example, write about the things you're grateful for. Or write every day about something good that happened to you. By focusing on the positives, and not just the negatives, you might realize that things aren't always as bad as they seem. This makes it easier to not overreact when things don't go right.

WATCH YOUR LANGUAGE

You know swearing, yelling, or insulting others doesn't help you solve any problems when you're mad. You know that kind of language usually makes you and the people you're talking to angrier. But did you know that cutting down on angry language in all parts of your life can help you be happier, calmer, and less angry in general? It's true.

The more frequently you cuss or use bad language, the angrier you are likely to be. Instead of calming you down, cursing can cause your anger to build. Swear words are angry words. Even if you use them only in private, where you can't hurt anyone or get yourself in trouble, they still can make you angrier. If you have problems with anger, it's probably best not to use these words.

AVOID THE BLAME GAME

It's easy to blame others for "making you angry." The reason it's easy is because it takes you off the hook. For example, "She shouldn't have said that. She really pissed me off." Blaming gives you an excuse to be angry at another person.

But this isn't really fair. Other people can't *make* you feel angry. They may do something you don't like, but you decide how to feel about it. Remember the ABC Theory (see pages 56–59)? It's your *beliefs* about things that control how you feel about them. If you believe people do things to make you mad, or to hurt or cheat you, then you are more likely to get mad. If you tend to blame others for your anger—or other problems—then you are likely to be angry more of the time. Taking responsibility for your feelings and avoiding blame is hard, but it can make you happier.

Here's something else blaming does: it causes arguments and fights. Nobody wants to be blamed by others. If you blame someone, he or she is probably going to get mad right back at you. Accepting responsibility for your own feelings can prevent a conflict.

Remember to use I-messages (see pages 34–35). Telling someone you feel upset at what he or she did doesn't lay blame. It just shares your feelings. This increases the chances that the other person will understand and not feel unfairly accused. You'll have a better chance of working through the situation peacefully.

PRACTICE EMPATHY

Empathy means being able to understand and feel the emotions of others. Being able to feel empathy is a very important skill for all people.

Empathy doesn't come easily for many people with anger problems. You get so wrapped up in how upset you are that you forget that the people you're mad at have feelings, too. They may be just as upset as you. They have good reasons (at least in their own mind) for acting the way they do.

If you're not very good at empathy, how can you get better? Here are two things to keep in mind.

Try to stay calm and try to understand why they did what they did to get you angry. —Boy, 14

Be the Other Person

Have you ever heard the phrase, "Walk in the other person's shoes"? That's empathy—feeling what it's like to be another person. Put yourself in that person's place. If you're fighting with your best friend, imagine you are your friend. Then ask yourself (as your friend), what am I feeling right now? Why am I feeling that?

Here's another example. Imagine your dad yells at you for not bringing home a carton of milk like he asked you to do. Your first reaction is to get mad right away and start yelling back. You think, "He always asks me to do stuff, and it's not fair that he should scream at me when I forget!"

Maybe it isn't fair for your dad to yell at you. But what if you looked at the situation from his point of view? Maybe he asked you yesterday and you promised to do it, so he feels like you ignored him. Maybe he had a bad day at work and was already grumpy when he got home. (That doesn't make it okay for him to take out his bad mood on you, but it does *explain* it.)

You have a better chance of resolving the problem without a fight if you can imagine how your dad feels. You will probably see that your dad wasn't trying to be a jerk. You might even be able to say, "Dad, I'm sorry I forgot. I'll go get some right now."

Use Reflective Listening

Reflective listening is a great skill because it shows the other person you're listening. And it actually helps you listen. It's also easy to do. Here's how it works:

Step 1: A person tells you how he or she feels.

Step 2: In a calm voice, you summarize for that person what he or she said.

Easy, right? Going back to our milk example, here's what you could have said to your dad when he got mad: "Okay, Dad, let me see if I understand. You're angry with me for forgetting to get the milk even though you reminded me. Then I made it worse by yelling back. Is that it?"

On hearing you say that, your dad now knows that he is understood. Being understood can help everyone calm down. It's a great way to put out another person's fire of anger. Then they'll be more likely to listen to your side of the situation. In turn, *you* are less likely to get mad, too.

LEARN HOW TO PROBLEM-SOLVE

Many times, anger comes out because people have a problem they can't solve. This is especially true if you and the person you're angry at tend to argue repeatedly over the same things.

The first step in solving the problem is to identify what it is. You and the other person might not agree at first on what the problem is. Don't try to figure out whose fault it is or who has been hurt the most. Just identify the problem.

Once you've agreed on the problem, it's time to brainstorm solutions. Brainstorming means coming up with as many possible solutions as you can. Do this with the person you're arguing with and anyone else you want to ask. Anyone can contribute ideas. Sometimes an adult like a parent or teacher can help a lot.

Don't Be a Know-It-All

There are two sides to every story. When discussing a problem or something that happened, you might be convinced that your memory is perfect. You think you remember word-for-word what you said and did and what the other person said and did. But unless you had a video camera, chances are that your memory is imperfect. Even if there was a witness, there's no guarantee that he or she would remember correctly either.

Scientists have proven that most people don't remember perfectly. Also, people tend to forget the things they did wrong. They often make up parts of a story without even realizing it. Even if you're sure you're right and the other person is wrong, what good does this do? Proving you were right doesn't help make a relationship stronger. So when you are giving your side of a story, it often helps to start off saying something like this:

"Danny, this is what I remember happening. Feel free to correct me if you remember it differently."

"Mom, maybe I'm wrong, but I really thought I told you I'd be late. I'm sorry if I didn't."

"It felt like you were yelling at me. That's why I reacted the way I did."

As long as you can admit that there is a chance that you were wrong and the other person is right, it will be much easier to work through problems or hurt feelings.

Write down all ideas on a sheet of paper without noting who came up with which ideas. Don't discuss the ideas as they are suggested. If you shoot down people's ideas as soon as you hear them, the spirit of cooperation will be destroyed. Even if you disagree with an idea, just write it down.

Once you have a list of ideas, look at each one and talk about it. Think of what would be good and what would be bad about each one. Cross off ideas that don't seem like they'll work. Narrow down your list to just a couple top choices, and then pick one to try.

For a solution to work, it has to work for *everyone*. That means you may have to **compromise.** Compromising means giving in a little on something you want in order to get something else you want. The other person will give in a little, too. Whatever idea you decide to try, give it some time to see how it works. If it doesn't work, go back and try another one. Problem-solving is a process, and it may take time. But it's the only way to resolve problems fairly.

***

The choices you make about your lifestyle affect everything you do, think, and feel. That's why it's called your *life*style. Making changes to it won't keep you from ever getting angry. But positive lifestyle choices will help you stay in control when you do get angry. They can even make you healthier and happier.

PART 3

ANGER AND RELATIONSHIPS

THE FIRE AT HOME: ANGER IN FAMILIES

I don't really get along that well with my mom, and my dad started acting differently toward me after their divorce. We used to be like best friends, but that changed after he found a new girlfriend. Mom seems too busy most of the time, and my dad yells at me for not calling him, even after I left two messages. Seems like with him, everything is my fault. It pisses me off because every time I tried to talk with him about it, he'd be too busy or tell me nothing's wrong.

Lately, home hasn't been so bad because me and my mom aren't yelling at each other. It's because I'm acting different—I don't start stuff with her anymore. Though she still does annoying things, I don't say everything I'm thinking because it would just tick her off. I just deal with it. It's mostly little things that can start a big argument. It helps that I'm hanging out with some of my older cousins. They make me laugh. They're like my big sisters. I watch how they act with their mom. She's just as annoying to them, but they act nice and make a joke of it.—*Girl, 14*

It makes me angry when my parents tell me to do something more than once that I already did or know to do.—*Boy, 18*

My anger has gotten worse lately. I can't help but talk back to my parents and I have to have the last word in any argument—even with my sister. The other night I had a fit because I couldn't order the dinner I wanted at a restaurant. I try to think about things in a more positive way, but it seems like I can only think about what will go wrong in the future. I complain a lot!—*Boy, 13*

My mom and my dad get on my nerves. Me and my sister get into fist fights a lot. When I'm really mad, I go into my room and slam my door.—*Girl, 13*

A family can be a source of great joy and support. But it can also be a source of anger. For many teens, it seems like family members have a special talent for ticking them off. Family members spend a lot of their time together, so there are many opportunities for conflict.

Maybe your family members squabble and argue. Maybe they take out their bad moods on each other. They might call each other names. They might even betray each other's trust. If people in your family have problems with anger, they might do all that before breakfast.

You may dream of the day you'll be able to move out on your own. But in the meantime, you can keep yourself out of trouble and be happier at home. Your family can learn to get along better.

HOW ANGER SHOWS UP IN FAMILIES

Many teens get angry at the way their parents treat them. They may feel their mom or dad doesn't respect them or trust them. Parents may:

- criticize you about your grades
- hound you about getting work or chores done
- question you about things in your life you prefer to keep private
- refuse to allow you to go places or see friends
- limit your use of computers, video games, cell phone, TV, or other things
- say no to something you really want to do

My parents make me mad when they make me clean the bathroom five times in a row because it's not good enough for them. If I speak up, they make me clean something else!—**Boy, 16**

Teens also get angry with their siblings. Maybe siblings borrow your things without asking. Or you think they get more attention, privileges, or gifts than you do. Perhaps you're jealous of your brothers or sisters because you think your parents like them better. Or you think they are more popular, better looking, more athletic, or smarter than you. That can be tough to handle.

One day I was angry with my sister and told her she should leave the house because I was tired of her, and she left. I regret saying that because she was really hurt.—*Girl, 17*

My older brother got mad because I was annoying him, so he punched me and pushed me into the wall.—*Boy, 16*

My sister got angry with me. She hit me and I hit her back because I was angry.—*Girl, 14*

Journal Anger in Your Family

How has anger affected your family? Who triggers your anger the most? Why? How do you think you contribute to anger problems in your family?

Along with the obvious ways, like yelling and arguing, anger often shows up in families in sneaky ways. Here are the two most common. Be on the lookout for these forms of anger and try not to let them into your family.

Passive-Aggressive Anger

Passive-aggressive anger shows up in families a lot, because kids and teens don't have much control in these relationships. Parents make the decisions and for the most part, kids have to do what parents say. It may seem risky or scary to be openly angry with a parent, because a parent can punish you. When it seems too hard to be honest about your anger, you may disguise it. You may or may not do this on purpose. The anger still burns like a fire, but now it's underground like a river of lava.

Find out about passive-aggressive anger on page 16.

Sometimes that lava spurts out above ground. You show your anger in little ways that you don't have to admit to. Examples include:

- "forgetting" to call your mom to let her know where you are
- telling your dad you'll clean the kitchen or do some other chore and then leaving without doing it
- giving your mom the "silent treatment" until she figures out you're mad at her
- not doing well in school as a way to get back at your mom or dad

As you learned in Chapter 1, passive-aggressive anger is a way to avoid responsibility for your anger. It's much healthier—and you'll solve more problems—if you let your family know, directly and respectfully, why you're mad.

Displaced Anger

People often do things unconsciously. That is, we do things without fully realizing why we're doing them. A good example is displaced anger. That's when you feel anger in a situation or toward a person, but you don't feel safe expressing your anger in that situation or to that person. So instead, you *displace* your anger: you take it out on someone else. This might be someone you're not angry with at all.

As with passive-aggressive anger, displaced anger is especially likely to occur in families. That's because you may feel more (or less) safe with your family than you do in other situations. Say you're mad at your teacher but you're afraid to tell him. But you're not afraid of your dad, so when you get home from school you blow up at him for something totally small and unimportant. Or maybe you're angry at your mom but you think if you tell her you're mad you might get grounded. So the next time your little sister gets on your nerves even a tiny bit, you scream at her. You've displaced your anger for your mom on your sister.

Remember to Talk

The most important thing to do in families is communicate. Talk to each other when you have a problem. Don't let anger build up or blow up. If you want ideas about tools for talking, go to page:

- 34 to read about I-messages
- 40 to read about controlling your language
- 70–71 to read about empathy and reflective listening

These tools help keep everyone respectful toward one another.

HOW TO KEEP ANGER FROM DAMAGING YOUR FAMILY RELATIONSHIPS

You can use any of the tools and strategies you've read about in this book to control your anger with your family. You can also keep using your journal to learn more about your anger and what works best for you. Here are a few additional strategies that work especially well in families.

Apologize

Many people, especially guys, find it hard to apologize. They may think it seems weak to apologize. But actually, the opposite is true: it takes a lot of guts to admit when you're wrong. And apologizing when you've hurt someone is the only way to let that person know you feel bad about what you did. It doesn't matter if you did it on purpose. Apologizing helps ease some of the hurt the other person feels because of what you did or said. It's a way of repairing relationships.

A good apology usually includes the following ingredients:

1. Saying the person's name

2. Letting the person know you're sorry

3. Repeating exactly what you did to hurt him or her

4. Letting the person know that you know it hurt

5. Making a promise to avoid hurting the person again in the future

It's best to be direct and simple. Here are some examples:

- "Dad, I'm really sorry I swore at you. I was mad you wouldn't let me go out, but I know that doesn't make it okay for me to swear. I'll work harder to keep my temper under control."

- "Jen, I'm sorry I blew up at you. I didn't like what you said to me, and I'm still upset about it, but I really didn't mean to yell like that. I know I scared you. Next time, I'll take a time out to cool down first. That will help make sure this won't happen again."

Don't promise anything you can't deliver. For example, saying you'll *never* do something again is hard to promise, especially if you've done it more than once before. If you say you'll never do something, and then you do it, your promises become meaningless. It's better to promise you'll *try*, since that's something you have control over. (But don't use "try" as an excuse. Work your hardest at changing your behavior so you won't hurt the other person again.)

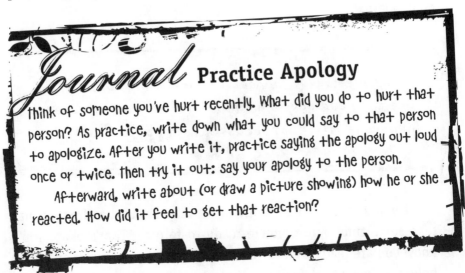

Journal **Practice Apology**

Think of someone you've hurt recently. What did you do to hurt that person? As practice, write down what you could say to that person to apologize. After you write it, practice saying the apology out loud once or twice. Then try it out: say your apology to the person.

After ward, write about (or draw a picture showing) how he or she reacted. How did it feel to get that reaction?

Forgive

"Why should *I* forgive? He's the one who acted like a jerk!"

"No way am I apologizing. She has to apologize first."

People find many reasons not to forgive. The reasons might be valid. For example, maybe it *was* the other person's fault. Maybe the other person *should* apologize first. Or maybe what the other person did is too awful to forgive. But if the other person doesn't apologize, you keep feeling angry and hurt. That bad feeling is like poison. It gets worse and worse. It may grow into hate.

Forgiving is the best way to get rid of the poison. It's a way of choosing not to feel lousy.

If someone hurts you, that isn't fair or right. And forgiving can't make it fair or right. It won't undo what was done. But here's what forgiving *can*

Read more about hate on pages 91–92.

do: it releases you from the hurt. It doesn't matter what the other person did. It doesn't matter if he or she deserves your forgiveness. When you forgive, you let go of the hurt and anger so you can feel good again.

> Once, when I was younger, I punched my cousin in the face, but he forgave me. Now, we're like brothers. I never hit anyone after that because I felt so bad.—**Boy**, *15*

If you're not used to forgiving, it may be hard at first. It may take some time before you're ready to forgive. That's okay. You'll know you are ready to forgive when it feels like too much energy to hold onto your hurt feelings. It starts to feel like a waste of time.

Here's how you do it. You don't have to say to the person, "I forgive you," though that can help. Forgiving means changing your attitude toward a person. You have to find a way to come to one of the following understandings:

■ the other person didn't mean to hurt you

or

■ the other person, due to his or her own problems, wasn't able to take your feelings into account at the time he or she hurt you.

For example, you may be angry at your dad for not keeping his promise to take you fishing when he said he would. But you forgive him because he is an alcoholic and can't always think straight because he is addicted to alcohol. It doesn't excuse his behavior, and it was still hurtful, but it helps you not take it so personally.

In some cases, it may be that the other person wanted to hurt you and didn't care about your feelings at all. When this happens, it can be a lot harder to forgive, though not impossible. People who intentionally hurt others and don't care about the consequences usually have something seriously wrong with them. They may be mentally ill or may have been treated very badly by people in their lives. That makes it hard for them to care about anyone other than themselves. Remember that forgiving helps you let go of all the anger and hurt you feel. You're no longer willing to dwell on it. You're ready to move on.

Here are a few tips to help you forgive:

1. **Apologize for any part you may have played in the problem.** This doesn't mean you take responsibility for the other person's actions. It just means you take responsibility for yours.

2. **Try to understand the other person's point of view.** (This is empathy. Read about empathy on pages 70–71.) Maybe the person felt justified in what he or she did to you. Maybe he or she was upset or under the influence of drugs or alcohol when it happened. Again, this doesn't excuse a person's behavior, but it may explain it.

3. **Decide if it would help to tell the other person you forgive him or her.** If so, plan out how you'll say it. Here's an example: "Mom, I know you're sorry for losing your temper with me the other day. It really hurt my feelings, but I know you had a stressful day. It didn't help that I forgot to take out the trash like I promised I would. I forgive you—and I'm willing to try harder to make things better between us." If sharing your wish to forgive seems to be a *bad* idea, or if it's not possible, consider putting your thoughts into a letter to the person. Even if you never send it, it can help get the feelings off your chest.

Imagine Tomorrow Never Comes

How would you treat your family members if you knew you'd never see them again? How would you feel if the last words you spoke to them were hateful? Thinking about this isn't pleasant, but this strategy can help you see a bigger picture when deciding how to treat others.

> One time I was really mad at my mom because she had messed something up on my computer. I actually made her cry. I felt really bad when that happened. —*Girl, 16*

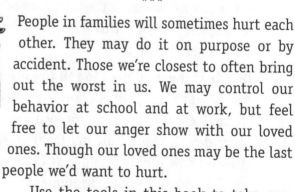

* * *

People in families will sometimes hurt each other. They may do it on purpose or by accident. Those we're closest to often bring out the worst in us. We may control our behavior at school and at work, but feel free to let our anger show with our loved ones. Though our loved ones may be the last people we'd want to hurt.

Use the tools in this book to take care of your family relationships. Remember to talk with each other. Learn to apologize and forgive. You have your family forever—don't forget that.

THE FIRE OF ROMANCE: ANGER IN COUPLES

It really pisses me off when my girlfriend is out with her "guy friends" and won't return my text messages or calls. Then I hear from my friends that she was flirting with a bunch of guys. She says it's not serious and that she only wants me, but I'm not so sure. When I bring it up, she starts yelling that I don't trust her and that leads to an argument. Sometimes I grab her to shake some sense into her, but that just makes it worse. My last girl dumped me because of this and I don't want it to happen again.—**Boy**, *18*

One time my ex-boyfriend wouldn't be affectionate toward me, and it hurt me, but I didn't say anything because I knew he was mad.—*Girl*, *15*

Me and my girlfriend constantly argue. We say what we know will hurt each other, because we're so angry.—**Boy**, *16*

My boyfriend makes me mad. He's also the person I talk to when something else makes me mad.—*Girl*, *18*

Being a teen can be fun, exciting, and . . . complicated. That's especially true when it comes to dating. The feelings you have for people you date are usually intense. They can also be confusing.

Because romantic relationships are so intense, it can be hard to make them work. It's easy to get hurt or angry. After all, you're putting your heart in your partner's hands. When you're dating someone, you open yourself up in ways you don't in other relationships. You might share some of your most personal feelings and secrets with the other person. The other person does the same, and you feel closer as a result. But the closer you feel to people, the greater their ability to hurt you.

HOW ANGER SHOWS UP IN RELATIONSHIPS

There are a few big reasons why people in relationships get angry. Cheating on each other or telling each other's secrets are two of the biggest. And there is often a lot of anger between people who break up. But even the healthiest relationships have conflict. Over time, problems will occur. It's normal to disagree over issues such as how much time you spend together, what you do when you're together, and who you hang with when you're apart. How you deal with these problems can make the difference between staying together and breaking up.

Here are common triggers for anger in romantic relationships:

- Your boyfriend doesn't call when he says he will.

- Your girlfriend ignores your phone call or text message.

- You see your boyfriend talking to another girl.

- You catch your girlfriend in lies about where she's been.

- Your boyfriend dumps you and doesn't have the guts to tell you face-to-face, but breaks up with you by email or through someone else.

- You feel your girlfriend is spending too much time with her girlfriends.

Most of these triggers have to do with trust. Someone breaks your trust, or you *think* they broke your trust. Some of the biggest anger-related problems that show up in relationships are **jealousy, passive-aggressive anger,** and **hate.**

Jealousy

Perhaps the biggest source of anger in relationships is jealousy. At first, some people might like the fact that their partner is jealous. They think it means he or she cares. This may be true. But over time, jealousy can turn into controlling behavior.

Jealousy is a mixture of insecurity, fear, and anger. You are insecure in your relationship with the person. You're afraid he or she may leave you for someone else. And you're angry with your partner or anyone else you see as a threat to your relationship.

People act with jealousy to try to keep a relationship together. But jealousy rarely brings people closer together and often breaks them apart. Beating up every person who talks to your significant other won't make your relationship any stronger. Attacking someone who talks to your date isn't going to keep him or her from talking to other people if he or she chooses to.

When jealousy gets to be too much, the person you're afraid of losing eventually leaves you. Your partner leaves not because he or she became interested in someone else, but because your jealousy was smothering.

The best ways to keep jealousy out of your relationship are to:

Not keep secrets. Let your partner know who you spend time with. Don't exclude your partner, and he or she will grow to trust you more. Keeping secrets from your partner usually is unhealthy in relationships.

Accept that you can't control others. Remember that you can't force someone to stay with you—he or she has to *want* to be with you. The way to make this more likely is to be the best partner you can. That means letting your partner have outside friends and interests. It means not trying to control him or her. If your partner is going to be unfaithful, it will happen no matter what you do. And if it happens, perhaps he or she isn't the person for you. It's better to find that out now instead of months or years later.

Passive-Aggressive Anger

Just like in families, passive-aggressive anger is common in romantic relationships. You may not want to risk being openly angry with your partner because you don't want to have a fight.

When you feel that way, you may disguise your anger. You show it in little ways that you don't have to admit to. Common examples of passive-aggressive anger in romantic relationships include:

Find out about passive-aggressive anger on page 16.

- "Forgetting" to call your girlfriend when you're out with friends because you don't want her to bug you about it

- Making plans to see your boyfriend, then backing out at the last minute and blaming your mom or dad for not being able to see him (when it's really you who doesn't want to see him)

- Not answering your girlfriend's calls to punish her after you just had a fight

- Flirting with other guys just to make your boyfriend jealous and see if he really cares about you

Remember that passive-aggressive anger usually makes things worse. It shows little respect for your partner and can be the beginning of the end of your relationship. It's always healthiest to be open about your feelings, even if it seems hard.

Hate

Hate is a feeling of extreme dislike and anger toward someone. Saying you hate someone is one of the angriest things you can say. Most anger eventually cools and goes away. But hate can last a lifetime. When you hate someone, you are unwilling to ever forgive that person for hurting you. You are unwilling to let go of your anger.

Hate usually drains a lot of your time and energy. You can't stop thinking about how much you hate the other person. You might even think about how you're going to get revenge. All these negative feelings can cause you emotional and physical stress. You keep focusing on your hurt, which makes it hard for you to ever heal from it. So hate ends up hurting you a lot more than it does the person you hate. That person is just fine, while you boil with negative feelings.

What does hate have to do with romantic relationships? Hate is an intense feeling, just like love. Sometimes people in a relationship say they hate each other. They might really mean it, or they might not. Sometimes, by holding onto their anger, they are also

Violence in Relationships

Because romantic relationships can be so intense, sometimes anger can lead to violent behavior. Examples include hitting, slapping, kicking, punching, scratching, and threatening. Another example is physically forcing someone to do something, including sex. If you feel your anger might lead to violence, it's important to get help right away, before you end up hurting someone you care about. You could even get arrested. If you're the one being hurt, you may need help putting a stop to it. Your partner may feel sorry after hurting you and promise never to do it again. But unless he or she gets help, the behavior is likely to happen again.

If you're in a violent relationship, whether you're hurting someone else or you're the one being hurt, talk to a trusted adult or professional. Call the National Domestic Violence Helpline at 1-800-799-SAFE (1-800-799-7233). You can also learn more at their Web site, www.ndvh.org/help/index.html. Click on "Info for Teens."

holding onto caring feelings for their partner. Breakups can also cause hate. People may feel so hurt after a relationship ends that they feel hate for their ex.

Maybe you've heard of a love-hate relationship. This is when you bounce back and forth between having those two feelings for someone. You love them when things are going well. But if they do something wrong in your eyes, you hate them. This makes it hard to get along consistently. If you tell someone you hate them, when really you're just very angry, that hurts deeply. Your partner isn't likely to forget what you said and this damages your relationship.

Here are some signs your anger may be turning into hate:

- You often think about the person you're angry at.

- You burn inside when someone even mentions the person's name.

- You feel a need to tell others how you were hurt, wanting them to feel your anger, too.

- You start seeing yourself as completely innocent and the other person as totally at fault, instead of admitting your role in the problem.

- You often think of ways to get revenge.

- You feel intense anger weeks and even months later.

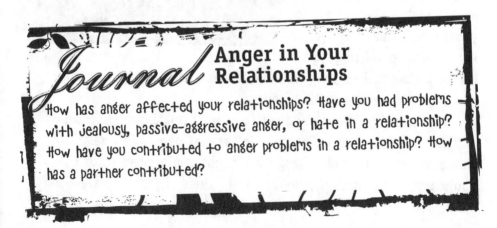

Journal: Anger in Your Relationships

How has anger affected your relationships? Have you had problems with jealousy, passive-aggressive anger, or hate in a relationship? How have you contributed to anger problems in a relationship? How has a partner contributed?

Hate doesn't go away easily. It's hard to let go of such an intense feeling. The best way to free yourself from hate is to forgive (see pages 83–85).

HOW TO TELL IF ANGER IS DESTROYING YOUR RELATIONSHIP

A well-known counselor and researcher, John Gottman, has studied couples to find out why some stay together and others don't. He found four major behaviors that predict whether couples will stay together. He calls them "The Four Horsemen." They are **criticism, contempt, defensiveness,** and **stonewalling.** If one or more of these behaviors occurs in your relationship, chances are it is in trouble.

Criticism

Gottman defines criticism as attacking who a person is rather than complaining about a specific behavior.

"You're such a jerk."

"You don't care about anyone but yourself."

"You never listen to me."

If you say something like that, you are attacking a person's character, not his or her actions. Calling your partner a jerk implies that's all he or she is. A better way to talk about disagreements is to be specific about what upsets you. Remember to use I-messages (see page 34) to help keep the focus on how you feel.

For example: "I felt really upset when you didn't call me last night after you said you would." This is better than saying, "You don't care about me" or "You never call when you say you will." Sentences like these criticize the person.

Criticism is often the first of the four horsemen, and can lead to the other three.

Contempt

When you have contempt for someone, you think you're better than him or her. You put yourself on a higher level than that person. The person disgusts you. Contempt usually comes out in sarcasm, name-calling, criticism, eye-rolling, sneering, mockery, and hostile humor. When someone is treated in these ways, they feel worthless.

If you can, avoid contempt the same way you avoid criticism. Make a complaint about a specific behavior that upsets you, but don't act as if the other person is lower than you.

Defensiveness

Being defensive is denying your behavior or making excuses for it. It can also be attacking back when someone accuses you of something. For example, imagine your girlfriend accuses you of flirting with another girl. Examples of defensive reactions would be:

- "I didn't do anything." (Denying it.)
- "I just needed to borrow a pencil. I barely even talked to her." (Making excuses for it.)
- "You don't trust me. You're the one with the problem." (Attacking back.)

A better reaction, one that is not defensive, might be: "Yes, I talked to her, but that doesn't mean I have feelings for her. Why don't you come over next time and I'll introduce you. That way you won't feel left out."

Stonewalling

Stonewalling is when you refuse to talk about problems. You may act like the problems don't exist. You avoid a fight, but you also avoid talking to your partner. You may stare at the ground or out the window when your partner tries to talk about a problem.

Stonewalling is usually the last of the four horsemen. Guys tend to stonewall more often than girls. As I hope you know by now, it is always better to talk about your problems than to ignore them.

Journal **The Four Horsemen**

Which of the four horsemen (criticizing, contempt, defensiveness, and stonewalling) have you experienced in your relationships? Has it come more from you or from your partner? What can you do to get over these problems?

HOW TO KEEP ANGER FROM RUINING YOUR RELATIONSHIPS

You can use any of the tools and strategies you've read about in this book to control anger in your romantic relationships. As with any relationship, the most important thing is to communicate. That means talking to your partner when you have a problem. Take a time out if you feel anger building up. To learn about some of the most important tools, go to page:

- 34 to read about I-messages
- 40 to read about controlling your language
- 70–71 to read about empathy and reflective listening
- 82–83 to read about apologizing
- 83–85 to read about forgiving

These tools help you and your partner be respectful of each other.

There's one other thing that can be especially useful in romantic relationships: **agree to disagree.** Sometimes, when arguing with your partner, you just can't come to an agreement. If you keep arguing, chances are you'll both get more and more angry. If you've tried hard to understand each other's point of view, maybe it's time to agree to disagree. You can say:

- "I guess we see it differently."
- "We'll have to agree to disagree on that for now."
- "I don't see it that way, but from the way you see it, I can understand why you're so upset."

This helps stop the argument. Sometimes, that's the most important thing.

* * *

Feeling rejected or hurt by a partner is one of the most upsetting things you may deal with in your teen years. If you talk openly about problems, you'll have a better chance to keep your relationships going.

FIRE AND FRIENDS: ANGER AMONG PEERS

My best friend was mad at me because I didn't call her back and she posted things on Myspace about me that I didn't want anyone to know. —*Girl*, 15

Me and my friend were both mad at each other. We got into a fight but afterwards we were friends again. —**Boy**, 15

My best friend ended up hooking up with my ex-boyfriend and didn't even tell me. I had to find out from another friend. I couldn't believe she didn't have the guts to tell me herself and lied about who she was spending time with. Now we're not speaking. —*Girl*, 17

My best friend gets mad and goes off on me, and I'll feel hurt and then we just start to cry together. Then we get over it. —*Girl*, 15

Your relationships with friends can be as intense as your relationships with family or dating partners. Sometimes, teens feel closer to their friends than to anyone else. If you work at your friendships, they can last a lifetime. But problems can come up that lead to fights and anger, just like they do in romantic relationships.

WHAT LEADS TO ANGER IN FRIENDSHIPS

Just like romantic relationships, friendships require a lot of trust. Good friends open themselves up to each other. They know each other's secrets. If a friend betrays your trust, it can be very painful. But even strong friendships have their problems. Anger often comes up when friends gossip, tell each other's secrets, are competitive, tease each other or call each other names, or can't balance time between friends and romantic partners.

Gossip

Many people gossip, including many teens. Gossiping is spreading rumors about people that may or may not be true. The rumors often let the gossiper feel power, control, or a sense of belonging. Gossip is often told to hurt others or get back at them.

It's easy to see how gossip can lead to anger. You may get mad if people gossip about a friend of yours. It's natural to get angry if people gossip about you. And you may get especially mad—and hurt—if you find out a good friend has been talking about you behind your back.

With gossip, it's best to listen to your feelings. If it feels mean or sneaky to be telling a story about someone, it probably is.

Keeping Secrets

One of the great things about having friends is that you have someone to talk to. It feels good when someone listens to you and really cares. You may talk about problems or successes. Maybe you tell a friend your secret desires or goals. You may even admit to funny or embarrassing things that have happened to you.

Sharing personal information brings people closer together. But it also can be risky. When a friend tells your secrets to others, you feel angry and hurt. You don't know who to trust.

Does this mean you should never tell anyone anything? Of course not. If you never tell a friend anything personal, you'll never have close relationships. But it's smart to be careful with your secrets. Make sure you can trust the person you tell secrets to. And if a friend trusts you with a secret, keep it secret!

Competitiveness

Being competitive in sports or games is usually healthy. It helps you do your best. But competing with friends often causes problems. Besides sports and games, friends are often competitive about grades and attracting dates.

Being competitive can be fine in friendships. It can even be a lot of fun. But when competition leads to jealousy or resentment, it can easily lead to anger, too.

Teasing and Name-Calling

Teasing and name-calling are common in middle school and high school. You may get teased for how you look, the way you talk, the things you do, or the friends you have. If a friend is teasing you, the best thing to do is be honest. Tell your friend how you feel about the teasing or name-calling. Maybe your friend is just trying to be funny. He or she might not realize it really bugs you. If that person is really your friend, he or she will quit.

Some people tease or bully because they want to feel strong. They hope to make you feel bad. They want you to react to their teasing with anger or frustration. The best thing to do if you're being teased is to not let them get that payoff. Don't show any anger or frustration. Don't let them know it bothers you.

Walking away or ignoring the teasing may work. If that doesn't seem like enough, you can do other things to make teasing less fun for the teaser. One way is to shrug it off and say something like "Whatever" or "That's fine." This way, you end the conversation. There's nothing left to talk about.

Another thing that works is asking stupid questions about the insult. Start your questions with who, what, when, where, why, or how. For example, imagine someone calls you a loser. You can give any or all of these responses:

- What do you mean?
- How do you know?
- How did that happen?
- Why should I care?
- Why do you care?
- Why are you saying that?
- What's your point?
- When was that?
- Where did you hear that?
- Who are you?

Act as if you're really puzzled or confused by the teaser's comments. Asking one silly question after another, without raising your voice or losing your cool, puts you in control. The key with saying "whatever" and with asking questions is to remain calm and not defend yourself. Don't tease back or show any anger. You will drain the fun out of teasing so the teaser doesn't want to do it any more.

Balancing Time Between Friends and Dating Partners

One common problem with friendships is balancing your time with friends and your time with your partner. It's natural to want to spend a lot of time with a partner, especially a new partner, because it's so exciting. But your closest friends may be hurt by this. They may feel left out. Sometimes you may feel torn between feelings for your friends and feelings for your partner. Remember that your friends deserve your time and respect, just like your partner does.

HANDLING ANGER WITH FRIENDS

As with other relationships, the most important thing is communication. Talk to your friends about any problems you have. If you think something is bothering them, ask. If they ask if something is wrong with you, be honest. Tell them how you feel and what you'd like them to do differently. Don't pretend nothing is wrong if that's not true.

To learn more about some of the most important tools for communicating, go to page:

- 34 to read about I-messages
- 40 to read about controlling your language
- 70–71 to read about empathy and reflective listening
- 82–83 to read about apologizing
- 83–85 to read about forgiving

These tools help you and your friends be respectful of each other. Here are some other ideas:

- Be clear on what you expect from friends. If you want to tell them a secret or something very personal, ask if you can trust them not to tell anyone.

- Don't let your anger build up. For example, if you're feeling jealous of a friend, say so. Your friend may have no idea. Once the person knows how you feel, he or she has a chance to behave differently.

- If one of your close friends starts ditching you to spend time with a new boyfriend or girlfriend, speak up. Tell your friend you miss hanging out.

- Remember that friends sometimes hurt each other's feelings. You can't expect things to be perfect all the time. If a friend apologizes for hurting you, and you can tell he or she means it, accept the apology and let it go.

- Be willing to listen to your friends if they have complaints about how you've treated them. It may be hard, but try not to get defensive. Thank them for letting you know. If you've hurt them, even unintentionally, don't be afraid to apologize. It's the quickest way to repair any relationship.

Relationships with teachers or coaches can be complicated, too. You may relate to these people as part friend and part parent. Things may go well when you're talking on a friend-to-friend level. But when they start telling you what to do, you may react negatively. The same guidelines apply to these relationships as any other. Be open about what is bothering you. Use the communication tools that are in this book.

Think of all your relationships—with family, romantic partners, friends, and others—as pieces of wood. Anger outbursts are like nails you drive into the wood. Even after you remove the nails (the outbursts end), holes remain in the wood. Apologizing can help fill the holes, but the wood is never as strong as it once was. And over time, if you put enough holes in the wood, eventually the wood crumbles and there is nothing left.

Journal

Anger in Your Relationships

Anger can damage all sorts of relationships. Sometimes, the damage can't be undone. People can only be hurt so many times before they decide it's not worth it and their life is better off without you.

Take an honest look at how anger has affected your relationships. Think about all your relationships: romantic, family, friends, even coaches and teachers. In your journal, answer each of the following questions:

1. How has my anger pushed away people I care about?

2. Have I lost any friends because of my anger problems?

3. Are people scared of me because of my anger?

4. How many people, whom I don't particularly like, have been hurt by my anger?

5. Has anyone ever broken up with me because of my anger?

6. Have I broken items that belonged to others out of anger?

7. Has anyone ever been inconvenienced by my anger (like having to repair something I've broken, bail me out of jail, or take me to court)?

After you have answered these questions, think about which ones have affected you the most.

PART 4

BURNING ISSUES

Growing up was hard for me. My dad was an alcoholic and often put me and my mom down. He'd call me lazy, stupid, and fat. He destroyed my self-esteem. He didn't understand that having ADHD made it harder for me to do well in school. I'd get mad at him, but also at my mom who put up with his behavior. I started using drugs myself and going out with any guy who would have me, just to prove to myself that somebody wanted me. But my anger started building and getting out of control. Mostly, I'd take it out on my mom—yelling at her, ignoring her, going out whenever I wanted. A couple of times I'd stand up to my dad, but I was too scared to keep doing it because you never know what he'd do when he's drunk. Counseling helped me realize that I was treating my mom the same way my dad treated me, and that wasn't fair to her. I learned to speak up for myself in a respectful way and once I did, my relationship with my mom improved. I still get mad at her for letting my dad treat us so badly, but now we talk about it when it starts upsetting me.—*Girl, 17*

Now that I'm on medication for depression as well as ADHD, I can laugh a bit more. But I still get pretty mad—I still have a long way to go.—*Boy, 13*

I used to cut myself but I got help with that. Now I have a psychiatrist and a journal.—*Girl, 13*

Mental health experts believe 1 out of every 5 teens has some kind of **mental disorder.** A mental disorder is when someone's feelings, thoughts, or behaviors seem unpredictable and hard to control, and when they get in the way of normal living a lot of the time. Examples include ADHD and depression.

If you have a recurring anger problem, there's a good chance you have one or more of the mental disorders discussed in this chapter. That doesn't mean you're "crazy"! It just means your brain works differently compared to others. Or perhaps you've had to deal with some really tough situations, which can cause disorders such as depression or anxiety.

If you have any mental disorders, it's important to get treated for them. (It's not unusual for someone to have more than one disorder.) Besides the problems mental disorders cause on their own, they can also make controlling your anger more difficult. Most teens in detention centers or jails have a mental disorder. For many of them, it was their anger that led them there.

Only a mental health professional can diagnose you with a mental disorder. If you think one or more of the disorders discussed in this chapter describes you, talk to a parent, counselor, or doctor. They can help get you evaluated by a psychologist or other professional. Only a professional can say for sure if you have a disorder.

If you are diagnosed with a disorder, you can begin getting treatment. Treatment for most of these disorders involves counseling, medication, or both.

ATTENTION DEFICIT HYPERACTIVITY DISORDER (ADHD)

People with ADHD have trouble being still, paying attention, and making good decisions. They may have trouble focusing on school-work or behaving in class. And they may have trouble getting along with adults and other teens.

There are three main types of ADHD:

- People with **Primarily Inattentive Type** have trouble paying attention. They get easily distracted, lose or misplace things, and are disorganized.

- People with **Primarily Hyperactive-Impulsive Type** are often fidgety or overactive. They may have trouble sitting still, tend to interrupt others, and are impulsive (they make bad decisions because they don't think about the consequences).

- People with **Combined Type** have both Inattentive and Hyperactive-Impulsive problems. They have problems paying attention, are hyperactive, and are impulsive.

If you have ADHD, chances are you get angry quickly without thinking about how you express it. Your anger usually doesn't last very long, and you may regret your actions later. You might also be impatient and easily frustrated. Having to wait before doing what you want to do can be hard for you. School is likely frustrating for you, which can add to your stress and contribute to anger prob-lems. Keeping track of assignments, staying focused in class, and completing homework on time are often difficult.

OPPOSITIONAL DEFIANT DISORDER (ODD)

People who have ODD are highly uncooperative, hostile, and defi-ant. They tend to argue with adults and peers a lot. They may not even care about winning an argument, just about having one. Here are some common symptoms of ODD (people with ODD probably won't have *all* of these symptoms):

- responding "no" whenever parents or others in authority ask them to do something

- losing their temper easily

- being easily annoyed

- annoying others on purpose

- blaming other people for their own mistakes

- wanting to get revenge on people who they think have done them wrong

- not wanting to compromise or negotiate; getting their way is more important than getting along with those they care about

If you have ODD, these symptoms create many problems in your relationships with others. Defiant behavior can be very frustrating for parents, teachers, friends, and partners. ODD also makes handling your anger more difficult. If you blame others for your problems, it's hard to take responsibility for your problems.

Many people with ODD have other disorders, too, such as ADHD or bipolar disorder (see page 112). These can make ODD worse. But getting help for other disorders can help with ODD symptoms.

CONDUCT DISORDER

People with conduct disorder violate the rights of others, over and over again. That includes breaking the law and injuring others. They see no problem with hurting others or breaking rules or laws. Symptoms include:

- bullying others

- starting fights

- using a weapon to threaten or hurt others

- being physically cruel to people or animals
- robbing or stealing from others
- destroying property
- setting fires with the intent to cause harm
- breaking into homes
- running away
- lying or conning others
- forcing someone into sexual activity

If you have conduct disorder, you may not feel guilty about these symptoms. For that reason, you don't have much motivation to control your behavior. Your conscience, which is your sense of right and wrong, doesn't work well. Thinking about the consequences of your actions may be the best way to keep your behavior under control. Most people with conduct disorder eventually get in trouble with the law because of their symptoms.

DEPRESSION

People who are depressed feel sad or irritable a lot of the time. They usually don't feel like doing much of anything, including schoolwork or chores, or even going out with friends. Things that used to be fun don't interest them as much. Other symptoms of depression include:

- sleeping too much or too little
- eating too much or too little
- being tired a lot and not having the energy to do much of anything
- difficulty concentrating or making decisions
- feeling worthless or having low self-esteem
- feeling hopeless

In more severe cases, depressed people may have thoughts of killing themselves. They may even attempt it.

If you're depressed, your anger problems most likely take the form of having a short temper and getting easily irritated. This tends to be more true for boys than for girls. You may want to be left alone and get angry when others try to get you to come out of your shell. Some psychologists say that depression is anger turned inward. Instead of blowing up at others, you attack or criticize yourself for all your faults, real or imagined. Unfortunately, this just adds to your depression and makes you feel worse.

If you are thinking of hurting yourself in *any way*, talk to someone RIGHT AWAY about it. These are serious thoughts, and they mean you need help now. Talk to a parent or another adult you trust. If you have a counselor, try to contact him or her. If no one is around, call 911 and tell the operator you are having thoughts of killing yourself.

You can also call one of the following organizations—seven days a week, 24 hours a day—and someone will help you. The calls are free. Or check their Web sites to learn more.

Covenant House Nineline
1-800-999-9999
www.nineline.org

National Hopeline Network
1-800-784-2433
www.hopeline.com

Thoughts about suicide will pass (especially with proper help). But suicide is permanent.

BIPOLAR DISORDER

Bipolar disorder is sometimes called manic-depression. That's because people with bipolar disorder often have severe mood swings. They go from very depressed to **mania,** often in a matter of seconds. Mania is when people feel extremely happy, irritable, or energetic—or all three. When you experience mania, you are **manic.**

Symptoms of depression are the same as listed in the previous section. Symptoms of mania include:

- not needing much sleep
- feeling a surge of uncontrollable energy
- feeling that one's thoughts are racing too fast
- having explosive anger outbursts or tantrums, which can last for a long time
- not being able to focus
- feeling better than everyone else
- being more talkative than usual or not being able to stop talking

Sometimes, people in a manic state will do dangerous or risky things they normally wouldn't do. Examples include engaging in sexual behavior, gambling, or drug use.

People with bipolar disorder often have big problems controlling their anger. Anger outbursts can be triggered by minor things. A person may curse, yell, hit, or destroy property. These outbursts are called rages. They can last for an hour or more. After the rage has passed, the person may feel bad for what he or she did. Some people don't even remember what they did while in a rage.

SUBSTANCE ABUSE AND DEPENDENCE

Substance abuse is when people use alcohol or other drugs, such as marijuana, so much that it causes problems in their ability to function. Substance abuse may affect their grades or cause problems at home. People may get into fights or legal trouble as a result of substance abuse. Driving a vehicle while under the influence of a substance can also be a sign of substance abuse.

Substance abuse can lead to substance dependence. People who are dependent may need more of the drug or alcohol to get high. They may not feel the effect of the drug as much if they keep using the same amount. Another symptom of dependence is withdrawal—a feeling of discomfort, even pain, or other physical symptoms when someone stops using the drug or alcohol. People who are dependent use more than they planned or use for a longer time. They may want to stop, but they can't. Their bodies start craving the drug and its effects. They spend a lot of time trying to get the drugs or recovering from the drug's effects. Finally, they give up activities they used to enjoy because of their drug or alcohol use.

People with anger problems may turn to alcohol or drugs to cope with their feelings. When high on marijuana, for example, things they felt angry about may seem to melt away. Alcohol or other drugs can also help them forget about their problems temporarily. While this may seem like a good solution, the problems always return. More importantly, by relying on drugs or alcohol to handle their problems, people don't learn to handle them on their own. This can keep them from growing up into responsible adults. Finally, using alcohol when under age or using illegal drugs can get them in trouble with the law.

If you are abusing or are dependent on alcohol or drugs, it's very important that you get help. The U.S. Department of Health has a phone number you can call to get information and help. The Alcohol and Drug Information hotline is 1-800-729-6686. Your school guidance counselor can find resources in your area. Some schools even have support groups that meet at school. See pages 66–67 for more information about drug and alcohol abuse.

EATING DISORDERS

Eating disorders are unhealthy eating patterns. They can lead to serious medical problems or even death. There are several kinds of eating disorders. One is **bulimia.** People with bulimia eat large amounts of food at once (called binge eating), but are able to maintain a normal weight. During binge eating, people feel out of control of their eating. After a binge, they will throw up or use laxatives to avoid gaining weight or may exercise hours a day to lose weight.

Anorexia is another type of eating disorder. People with anorexia are very underweight and afraid of gaining weight or think they're fat, no matter how thin they are. To get thinner, they eat as little as possible. Some people with anorexia also may engage in binge eating. Afterward, they often throw up, use laxatives, or exercise excessively to avoid gaining weight.

Still others eat so much that they gain lots of weight and become **obese.** They may get emotional comfort from eating. People with eating disorders usually try to keep them secret.

Problems with anger are often connected to eating disorders. People with anger problems may feel they have little control over their lives. So they focus on the one thing they feel they have the most control over, their eating. Eating disorders can also be a way of controlling others. They may force family members or others to pay a lot of attention to the person with the eating problem.

Eating disorders are very dangerous. If you don't maintain a healthy weight, your body organs cannot work properly and your bones become weak. You can die from starvation. Overeating and vomiting can damage your teeth and cause other health problems. Binge eating and being obese can cause you to develop diabetes and heart disease. It's very important to get help for eating disorders before it is too late.

For more information, check out the following resources:

- **National Eating Disorders Association:** www.edap.org
- **Anorexia and Related Eating Disorders, Inc.:** www.anred.com
- **The National Institute of Mental Health:** www.nimh.nih.gov/publicat/eatingdisorders.cfm

POST-TRAUMATIC STRESS DISORDER (PTSD)

People with PTSD have experienced or witnessed a traumatic event and are still affected by it for a long time afterward. Such events can include being in an accident, being attacked, or being abused. The symptoms usually show up a month or more after the event. People with PTSD may have flashbacks, which means they feel as if the traumatic event is happening all over again. They might also feel numb or be easily startled.

For teens, being physically or sexually abused or assaulted can lead to anger problems. Even being emotionally abused can lead to uncontrollable anger. For example, if a parent, caregiver, or even a sibling constantly puts you down, yells at you, calls you names, or makes you feel bad in other ways, it's natural to feel angry. When this happens over a period of months or years, the anger can build up and stick with you.

When you're carrying all that anger, it might come out at other times. This is especially likely when new situations remind you of the old traumatic ones. Even something small can cause you to blow up. The anger you feel isn't just from the new situation, but from feelings buried from the traumatic event, too.

For example, imagine a girl was physically abused by her father. Then imagine she and her boyfriend are playing around, wrestling, and suddenly she gets scared. She starts screaming at him to stop, even though he was just being playful. Her reaction might surprise her until she figures out where the anger is coming from.

Some people forget the traumatic event ever happened. They block it from their memory. This makes it especially confusing when they overreact to new situations. They may not be able to figure out why their reaction was so strong.

ASPERGER'S DISORDER

People with Asperger's Disorder have problems with social skills and social situations. They are usually loners and have trouble making friends. They have trouble reading social cues, such as body language, and are uncomfortable looking people in the eye. But Asperger's Disorder is more than just being shy. People with this disorder find dealing with others very confusing, and they don't seem to understand how to interact with others appropriately. They may also:

- be overly honest in ways that make others uncomfortable
- have trouble understanding humor
- behave in ways their peers think are "weird"
- be clumsy

Many people with Asperger's Disorder have a few intense interests. For example, they may be obsessed with baseball statistics, bus schedules, history, animals, or other topics. They may talk for a long time about these subjects without noticing if others are interested or even listening.

Anger problems are not a main part of Asperger's Disorder. But people with Asperger's Disorder are likely to be teased by others for being different. This can cause anger outbursts. People with Asperger's Disorder may express their anger in inappropriate ways. Learning better social skills and how to handle teasing more effectively can help. Talk to a parent, school counselor, or any adult you trust to get help with these things.

INTERMITTENT EXPLOSIVE DISORDER (IED)

People with this disorder have anger outbursts. During these outbursts, they become aggressive and can't control their impulses. They often end up hurting others or destroying property.

Usually, the outburst is completely out of proportion to whatever triggered it. It often involves physically hurting someone or destroying property. For example, imagine your mom says you can't go out on a school night. If you have IED, you might react by throwing the remote at your mom and breaking a mirror or kicking a hole in the wall.

Some people say they feel different right before an outburst. They feel tingly, their hands shake, their heart races, or their chest feels tight. They often feel rage or increased energy during the outburst. The outbursts can be very upsetting.

Not much is known about this disorder. It appears to be rare. Some people with IED feel fine between episodes. Others have anger problems.

SELF-INJURY

Some people feel so overwhelmed by negative feelings such as anger that they hurt themselves on purpose. The most common way they do it is by cutting themselves. They might use a knife, razor, fingernails, or other sharp object. Others may burn themselves.

Some people who injure themselves this way feel like it's the only way to get their angry feelings out. Others may be trying to punish someone they are angry with. Still others injure themselves because the physical pain distracts them from their emotional pain.

Self-injury can become addictive. People who do it may come to rely on self-injury to deal with their negative feelings. Self-injury can also be very dangerous. Some people who do it accidentally kill themselves, for example, by cutting too deeply.

Self-injury is not recognized as a mental disorder. But some people who injure themselves go on to develop Borderline Personality Disorder (BPD). BPD is a serious mental disorder. People with BPD have problems with unstable and intense relationships and moods. They have trouble controlling their feelings and impulses. Feeling intensely angry and having difficulty controlling their anger are big problems. People with BPD have trouble developing a consistent sense of who they are, and often feel empty inside.

If you have feelings of wanting to hurt yourself, tell someone. Ask a parent or other adult you trust to get you help.

* * *

Remember, only a mental health professional can tell for sure if you have a mental disorder. If you think you might be dealing with any of the disorders in this chapter, talk to an adult. A parent, teacher, guidance counselor, or other adult can help you get the professional help you need. Controlling any mental disorders you have will make it much easier for you to control your anger.

11

WHEN ANGER GETS YOU IN TROUBLE

My friend got suspended because some other person called him a bad name and he took his anger out on that person.—*Boy, 15*

My friend was so mad she threw a rock through a car window and the cops showed up. She had to go to court and she had to pay for the window.—*Girl, 16*

I rarely get into fights now, 'cause I see no point to it. I will throw stuff and I've punched a few holes in walls. Now that I have a daughter it's different. Sure, there have been times when I wanted to bust one of these females in the face, and the only thing that stops me is knowing that I could lose my daughter if I get into more trouble. I can't afford any more charges.—*Girl, 17*

Someone was messing with me and it made my boyfriend mad. He punched him and got charged with assault.—*Girl, 13*

My brother got mad at my other brother and they got into a fight. It was so bad my brother who started it went to jail for the night.—*Girl, 14*

I got mad at this kid at school and beat him up. I got suspended.—**Boy,** *17*

I know someone who got in trouble for not wearing his ID in school. He refused to put it on and cursed at the administrators and the police officer and was arrested.—**Boy,** *16*

My friend and a teacher got into a small fight, and suddenly my friend ran out of the class and hid in the bathroom while the teacher searched for him. Eventually, my friend came back, and after school he and the teacher talked it out.—Boy, 14

I got arrested because I got mad at my mom and I kind of beat the crap out of her. The cops said if I do it again then I go to a foster home.—Girl, 15

For many teens, problems with anger control can lead to trouble at home, at school, or with the law. For example, if your anger leads to a fight, you can get suspended or arrested. You can be arrested if you are using drugs or alcohol to cope with your angry feelings. You can even be arrested for disobeying a parent.

More than 2 million kids and teens were arrested in the United States in 2005. About 95,300 of those arrests were for violent crimes. About 418,500 were for crimes against property. For most young people who get arrested, dealing with the legal system is difficult and painful. It is often unfair. That's why it's so important to control your anger before you get in trouble. If you do get in trouble, it's helpful to know what to expect.

It is believed that 50 to 75 percent of all kids and teens who are arrested have a mental health disorder or other disorder. The most common disorders are conduct disorder, oppositional defiant disorder, bipolar disorder, substance abuse or dependence, learning disorders, and ADHD. That's why it is so important to get help for a disorder if you have one. See Chapter 10 for more information about these disorders, and Chapter 12 for more about getting professional help.

REASONS TO TRY TO AVOID LEGAL TROUBLE

No one wants to get in trouble with the law. You have to spend your personal time as well as your parents' time in court. You may have to spend money on attorneys and fines. You may have to spend time in detention. Besides these obvious reasons, there are other reasons to avoid trouble with the law.

The Fairness of the Legal System

It would be nice to believe that courts always operate fairly, but they don't. Lawyers, judges, and juries all make mistakes. People have biases that affect their judgment. For example, you can be targeted based on your race or gender. Research shows that racial profiling, in which black people are more likely to be stopped by police than white people, does exist in some areas. If you are African American, you may be at higher risk of being arrested, convicted, and put in detention. This is unfair, but it is a reality and something to consider when deciding whether to break the law.

You can also be falsely accused of a crime. If you are, the judge may believe the person accusing you. If you believe you have been unfairly convicted, you can appeal the decision (ask a higher court to reconsider the judge's decision). However, there is no guarantee that you will be found innocent. It will also cost you more money if you have an attorney.

Your Legal Record and Your Future

Another important factor to consider is how having a criminal record will affect you later in life. Once you have been charged and convicted of a crime, you will have a legal record. In some places, just being arrested, even if you aren't convicted, can result in your having a record. In some cases, your record will be sealed or destroyed when you finish serving your sentence. But in other cases, your conviction record may be kept for many years.

Some employers won't hire you if you have a record. For instance, imagine you are convicted of assault. If you apply to be a teacher, the school system may do a background check and decide not to hire you. The same may occur if you wish to join the military.

For first offenses, sometimes the court will grant you "youthful offender status." They will destroy your record after you turn 21 if you stay out of trouble for a certain amount of time. If you have done well and turned your life around, you may ask the court to destroy your record.

HOW PEOPLE GET IN TROUBLE WITH THE LAW

The most common reason people with anger control problems get into trouble with the law is because they hurt or threaten someone. Threatening to hurt someone, even if you don't actually do it, is called **assault,** and can get you arrested. Hurting someone physically is called **battery.**

Other common examples of illegal behavior include:

- **rape or attempted rape:** sexually assaulting someone

- **burglary:** stealing property from others

- **robbery:** stealing from someone directly by confronting him or her

- **vandalism:** intentionally destroying property that doesn't belong to you; you can also be arrested just for threatening to destroy property (like calling in a bomb threat)

- **arson:** setting fires on purpose

- **drug possession or distribution:** having or selling illegal drugs

People under the age of 18 can also be arrested for disobeying a parent. If the parent's rules are reasonable, kids and teens are required by law to follow them. Laws vary from state to state, but usually judges can order you to obey your parents. They can also order you to attend school, get counseling, take medication, and other things.

Severity of Crimes

Felonies are the most serious crimes. These include murder, assault, rape, stealing from a home, and other violent offenses. Punishment for felonies can range from probation to death. Juveniles (people under age 18) cannot be sentenced to death in the United States. Still, some juveniles can be tried as an adult. If you are tried as an adult, you can face many of the same punishments (including spending years in prison) as adults for the same crime.

Misdemeanors are less serious crimes, such as stealing. **Petty offenses** are illegal behaviors that don't qualify as a felony or a misdemeanor, such as not wearing your seatbelt. **Status offenses** are those that are illegal only because you're under 18 or under 21. These include smoking, possession of alcohol, running away, or being out past curfew.

Juvenile Detention and Prison

If you are sentenced to do time as a juvenile, you will probably be sent to a juvenile detention facility. There, you will live with other kids your age. Juvenile facilities can be violent. There may be gangs and dangerous individuals in there. Staff at these facilities don't always treat you fairly either.

If you're tried as an adult, you can be sentenced to prison. Prisons can be much more dangerous than juvenile facilities. The risk of being assaulted in a prison is much greater than in a juvenile facility.

YOUR DAY IN COURT

If you have been arrested, you will probably have to appear in court at a later date. Be sure to dress up on the day of your court appearance. It's smart to try to impress the judge. At the least, wear a dress shirt or blouse and dress pants or skirt. Guys should wear a tie. Wear nice shoes, too, not sneakers. You may believe it shouldn't matter what you look like. But whether it should or not, it does. The smart thing is to dress to impress.

When you get to court, a schedule will tell you which courtroom you'll be in. It will also tell you who your judge will be. In some cases, you will be scheduled to appear at a certain time. In others, you will have to show up in the morning and wait for your case to be called.

When it's your turn, family and friends will come with you into the courtroom. So will your attorney if you've hired one. Usually, the attorney for the plaintiff (victim) will start by describing what you are being accused of. Then you or your attorney will present your side. The judge will listen to both sides. The plaintiff's attorney may ask you questions. Your own attorney may do the same.

The judge also may talk to you directly and ask you questions. **Be sure to be respectful in your tone.** The judge has the power to decide what happens to you. Addressing him or her as "sir," "ma'am," or "your Honor" is always a good idea.

At the end of your hearing, the judge will decide whether he or she thinks you are guilty. In more serious cases, a jury (a group of citizens) may listen to your case and decide if you are guilty or innocent. If you are found guilty, the judge will decide what your punishment will be.

Plea Bargains

Does it make sense to admit to committing a crime, since this makes it more likely that you will have a consequence? If you deny you did anything wrong, there is a chance you will be found not guilty, even if you committed the crime. However, sometimes you will be given a lesser sentence if you agree to plead guilty. This is called a plea bargain.

A plea bargain can obviously help you if you think you will be found guilty. But there is another benefit to plea bargains. When you admit to hurting the victim, you allow him or her to heal. You also can help yourself. By admitting to the pain you caused, you might be more motivated to learn how to control your anger.

If you have committed a serious crime, such as assault, rape, or murder, you may be taken into custody on the spot to serve detention time. You may also be fined or asked to perform some type of **restitution** to make up for what you did wrong. Restitution may mean paying money to the victim or doing community service.

You might also receive a **suspended sentence**. This means you are given detention time, but you don't have to go to a juvenile detention center or to prison for the entire time. But if you get in trouble again with the law, you can be arrested immediately and you'll have to serve the rest of the sentence you were given.

PROBATION

Many teens who are convicted are put on **probation.** Instead of spending time in detention, you are given another chance to improve your behavior while the court monitors your progress. Besides simply staying out of trouble with the law, probation terms can include:

- keeping your grades up
- completing community service
- going to counseling
- getting and keeping a job

You may also regularly be tested for drugs, especially if your offense was drug related.

Probation can be supervised or unsupervised. If it is supervised, you will meet with a probation officer (P.O.) regularly. The P.O. will make sure you are staying out of trouble and meeting the terms of your probation. The officer can visit you at school, at home, or at work. You may be required to keep a curfew, such as being home by 7 PM on school nights and 9 PM on weekends. Your P.O. can check to make sure you're at home.

If your probation is unsupervised, you don't have to meet with anyone. You are just expected to stay out of trouble for the length of your probation. You may still have to follow certain rules while on unsupervised probation.

Probation can be definite, as in active for a specific period of time. It can also be indefinite, meaning that your P.O. can keep you on probation for as long as he or she thinks is necessary. In some cases, you can be kept on probation until you turn 21. If you do especially well while on probation, meeting all requirements and keeping out of trouble, your P.O. may be able to release you earlier than scheduled.

Here's a little more information on some of the common probation terms.

Community Service

This is a way of giving back to the community as well as a form of punishment. You may have to give talks to kids about your experiences, help out in a nursing home or animal shelter, perform charity work, pick up trash, help out at a church, or any one of a variety of services. You may be given as little as 10 hours or as much as 100 hours or more. It depends on the judge and on your crime. You do not get paid for your service. You will need proof that you completed your community service.

Drug Testing

If drugs or alcohol were involved in your crime, you will probably have to take periodic drug tests. Usually, you will be asked to give a urine sample as part of your meeting with your P.O. Often, you will be monitored. This means someone (of the same sex) will have to watch you pee into the cup to make sure that the urine is actually yours.

Drug testing can also be unscheduled. Your P.O. may call you at your home and insist that you show up in the next 24 hours to give a sample. If you don't show up, the P.O. can take that to mean you have continued to use drugs.

Some people think you can increase your chances of passing a drug test by drinking lots of water or using certain products that claim to "clean your system." There is no evidence that these products work. They may even be dangerous. Some drug tests are designed to detect the use of these chemicals. If you're caught using them, you can get in even more trouble. Your best bet is to not use drugs.

If you test positive for illegal drugs, you may be asked to enter a drug treatment program. If you refuse, you are breaking the terms of your probation. You will have to go back to court to explain your actions to the judge. The judge can send you to detention or add additional requirements to your probation.

Counseling While on Probation

Depending on the reason you were placed on probation, you may be required to attend counseling. Normally, counseling sessions are confidential, meaning your counselor must keep the things you talk about private. But it can be different when you are on probation. Some probation officers will respect your privacy, while others will check with your counselor to see how you are doing.

Be sure to talk to your counselor to find out how confidentiality will work for you. Most of the time, the P.O. only wants to know that you are attending, participating, and cooperating with treatment. If you do these things, and your counselor communicates that to your P.O., this may help your case. Of course, if you don't cooperate, your counselor will have to report that as well. Read more about counseling in chapter 12.

GETTING AN ATTORNEY

If your crime is serious, you may want to hire an attorney. An attorney will understand the system and can negotiate for you with the prosecutor. Your attorney can help with a possible plea bargain, which saves the time and expense of having to present your case in court.

If you cannot afford an attorney, you may ask for a court-appointed attorney. These are attorneys who have volunteered to represent clients with limited income. You should know that these attorneys are often paid very little for their work. As a result, they may be less motivated to put in much time on your case. A court-appointed attorney probably won't work as hard for you as an attorney you hire yourself.

Your discussions with your attorney are protected by what is called "attorney-client privilege." This means that your attorney has to keep his or her conversations with you private. It is best to be honest with your attorney. This helps the attorney defend you better.

* * *

Your best bet is to avoid the court system. Keep your anger under control and learn how to manage your outbursts so they do not result in breaking the law. That way you will not have to worry about defending your actions in court.

Unfortunately, for some people, it's not until they get in trouble with the law that they realize they need help with their anger. For them, the stress and hassle of legal trouble may help them find a reason to control their anger. Juvenile courts generally try to rehabilitate teenagers (help them get out of trouble and learn to fix their problems). Adult courts are more geared toward punishing people for their crimes. For that reason, it's important to learn to control your behavior while you are still young.

12

HOW TREATMENT CAN HELP

My counselor helped me see that I was turning my anger inward. Of course, the only person I was hurting was myself. He helped me learn to speak up for myself. —Boey, 17

Trying the ideas in this book can help a lot with controlling your anger. But sometimes, working on the ideas on your own isn't enough. You may need the help of a mental health professional. He or she can help you figure out why anger is such a problem for you and how to gain more control over your anger. If you have one of the disorders described in Chapter 10, you may need counseling and/or medication. In this chapter, you'll learn about counseling and medicine and how they can help.

COUNSELING

Counselors are trained professionals who can help you figure out why you are having problems and how to handle them. Maybe you are struggling with controlling your anger and you can't seem to improve on your own. If so, you and your family may decide that talking to a counselor will help. If you are in trouble with the law, a judge may order you to see a counselor. If your anger has caused problems at school, school officials can also require you to get counseling as a condition of returning to or staying in school.

There are several ways you might go to counseling, including **individual counseling, group counseling,** and **family counseling.**

Individual Counseling

In individual counseling, you meet with a counselor one on one. Counseling sessions are usually held once a week and last for 50 minutes. Your counselor will ask you questions like:

- What makes you angry?

- How do you react when you get angry?

- What strategies do you think might work to help you control your anger?

Together, you can come up with ideas that will help you. Then you can practice the ideas at home. Of course, you don't have to talk only about anger. Counselors also are trained to help you with other kinds of problems. Examples include your grades in school or your relationships.

Counselors have different types of training and may have different titles. Your counselor may be a psychiatrist, psychologist, licensed social worker, licensed professional counselor, or marriage and family therapist. Psychiatrists are medical doctors who have special training in using medications to treat mental disorders. Psychologists are trained to do psychological testing. This includes intelligence and personality tests. Testing can help when your counselor isn't sure if you have a disorder or what kind of treatment would help.

Group Counseling

If you are in trouble with the law as a result of anger problems, you may be referred to group therapy. In group therapy, you meet with a counselor and other teenagers who also have anger problems.

Some groups are structured and have a schedule of topics to cover for each meeting. You may have homework to do in between sessions. Other groups are more informal. Group members decide what to talk about.

You don't get to talk as much as you do in individual therapy, but you can learn from the other people. You listen to their problems and learn what worked for them. Group members also may give you feedback on how you're handling your problems. This can be hard to get used to at first. Try to remember that you're there to learn better anger control strategies. You'll get the most out of it if you're open to what others have to say.

Family Counseling

If anger is an issue in your home, family counseling may be helpful. In family counseling, you meet with one or more members of your family as well as with a counselor. Together, you work on how family members relate to each other.

For example, say your mom tends to yell at you to get you to do something. If this is an anger trigger for you, she can learn in family counseling to ask you in a calm voice. You, in turn, would agree to do what she asks without arguing. That way, everyone wins.

You can meet with your siblings, too. This may be helpful if you're having problems with one or more of them. Or maybe you want your brother or sister to join you because he or she might be helpful in your work to control your anger.

Confidentiality

Normally, what you tell your counselor is confidential. Your counselor is not allowed to share with others what you say without your permission. This may include your parent or parents. Laws vary by county, state, or country, so be sure to ask your counselor if you have questions.

There *are* times when your counselor may have to share information. These include:

■ If you threaten to hurt or kill yourself, your counselor will need to tell your parent so they can make plans to keep you safe.

- If you tell your counselor that you have physically or sexually abused a minor (a person under 18), your counselor must report this. He or she will report it to Child Protective Services or the police. It is against the law for your counselor to keep this information private.

- If you tell your counselor you are planning to kill someone, he or she will have to let the authorities know. This includes plans to do something like blow up a building, which can end up killing others.

- If you tell the counselor who you are planning to kill, your counselor may also have to try to contact the person you want to harm to warn him or her.

There may be other reasons your counselor will not be able to keep what you talk about private. Be sure to ask about your counselor's confidentiality policies. Find out before you share something if you are concerned that he or she may have to tell others.

Counseling Takes Time

It takes time for counseling to work. The amount of time depends on how well you get along with your counselor. It also depends on how willing you are to try out different ideas to handle your anger better. If you don't think counseling is helping, or if you disagree with the way the counselor is working with you, talk about your concerns with your counselor.

It's normal to be uncomfortable with your counselor sometimes, especially if he or she is pointing out your behavior in ways you aren't used to. The truth can hurt. But your counselor can't help you if he or she isn't honest with you about your behavior and how it affects others. If you've tried talking with your counselor about how you feel and it still doesn't seem like it's working, ask your mom or dad if you can try working with a different counselor.

MEDICATION

If you have been diagnosed with a disorder such as ADHD, depression, or bipolar disorder, you may be given medication to help with your symptoms. Medicines can help you handle frustrations without reacting so quickly. They can help you let go of things you're angry about more quickly. Many medicines have a calming effect. They may keep you from reacting so quickly or aggressively. Or they may help you think first before responding to your anger.

Different types of medicines are used for different disorders.

- **Antidepressants** can help with depression as well as anxiety. They make people less irritable, so things don't upset them as quickly. Antidepressants can also help with attention and impulse control.

- **Mood stabilizers** are used to treat bipolar disorder and sometimes depression. They help keep people from overreacting—from getting too energized and angry or from getting too depressed. They also help with anger control.

- **Stimulants** help the control centers of the brain work better. That helps people focus and control their impulses more effectively. Stimulants are prescribed for people with ADHD. They can help if your anger tends to be impulsive—you react too quickly without thinking.

- **Antipsychotics** can help control the manic symptoms of bipolar disorder (see Chapter 10 for more information). They can also help control a person's explosive anger outbursts that result in hurting others or destroying property.

Follow the Directions

If you are prescribed medication, be sure to take it exactly as the doctor prescribes. Usually, the instructions are on the bottle. Never take more than you are supposed to unless your doctor tells you to do so. Some medications are dangerous if you take more than the recommended amount. Don't drink alcohol or use illegal drugs while taking medication. Also, don't drive until you know the medicine doesn't make you sluggish.

Many medications have "side effects." These are symptoms the medicine can cause that are unwanted and distracting. Common side effects include:

- headaches
- stomachaches
- sleepiness
- eating less or eating more
- gaining or losing weight
- fatigue
- sleep problems

If any of these things happen to you (or anything seems different after starting a medication), be sure to let a parent (and your doctor) know right away to see if anything can be done to help. Usually, side effects get better with time.

Sometimes, medicine can make the symptoms you are trying to treat get worse. For example, it is possible that an antidepressant can make you more depressed. It can also make you angrier or even cause you to have thoughts about hurting yourself. If anything like this happens, have your mom or dad call your doctor immediately. These are dangerous reactions.

Many teenagers dislike taking medication. It makes them feel different. It can be a hassle to remember to take it at the right times. And the side effects can be a problem. If you have these concerns, be sure to be honest with your counselor and the doctor who is prescribing the medication. Ask any questions you have about medicines.

If you have concerns about medicine, perhaps you can agree to try it for a while to see if it actually helps. If you find a medicine that helps but has bad side effects, the doctor can often fix that. He or she can change the dose (how much you take), change the time of day you take the medicine, or switch you to a different medicine in the same category that might cause fewer side effects.

SCHOOL ACCOMMODATIONS

If you have a disorder such as ADHD, bipolar disorder, depression, or others, you may be able to get special help at school. You can also get help if your anger outbursts cause problems at school or get in the way of your ability to learn. Your school (along with you and your mom or dad) can come up with written plans to make changes at school. These changes will make it easier for you to learn. They are called **accommodations.** Since medication can also cause problems at school, you may need accommodations for that as well.

Depending on your disability, your accommodations may be an IEP (Individualized Education Plan) or a Section 504 Plan. Under both these plans, the school makes changes to help you. The changes might include:

- allowing you to leave the room to talk to your guidance counselor if you feel you're going to lose control

Omega-3 Fatty Acids

One natural way to help yourself with anger problems is to take omega-3 fatty acid supplements. Omega-3 fatty acids are types of fats that your body and brain need to work well. They are found in cold-water fish such as salmon. Many people don't get enough of them in their diet.

Research has shown that taking these supplements can reduce anger. In one study, prisoners convicted of violent crimes had lower levels of omega-3 fatty acids in their brains. Prisoners who took omega-3 supplements had lower levels of reported anger and violent behavior.

Taking fish oil supplements may also improve your physical health. Be sure to check with a parent and doctor before taking any supplements.

- allowing you to take a short break from your work

- reducing your homework load

- giving you an extra set of books for home if you have problems forgetting your books

- helping you organize your school materials

These changes can reduce your frustration in school. That can help you keep your anger under control.

Some schools have limited resources and may not be very quick to provide accommodations. You and your family may need to be persistent to get the help you need. This is your right.

A FINAL WORD

Anger is a normal emotion that can help motivate people to change situations they're unhappy with. The anger reaction has made it possible for humans to survive for more than a million years. But the fire of anger can hurt those close to us if it gets out of control. Anger can get us in trouble with the law. It can scare others away, which is the opposite of what most people want. And it can make you feel worse about yourself.

The good news is that there is a lot you can do to help you control your anger. Strategies such as getting exercise, taking deep breaths, and changing your beliefs about how things should be can help you stay calmer. With practice, these strategies can help improve your relationships with the important people in your life.

Once you learn to keep control of your anger, rather than letting it control you, you'll have a powerful tool. For example, using your anger constructively is one of the traits of a good leader. Anger can give you the motivation and energy to rally people to your way of thinking. Perhaps the most important reason to learn to use anger in a positive way is this: it's an effective way to let others know how you feel and to gain the respect you deserve.

THE BRAIN

BrainPlace

www.brainplace.com/bp

Learn more about brain imaging at the Web site of Dr. Daniel Amen. Click on the "Spect Imaging" icon to compare different brain images. The gallery contains brain images of a healthy person, a mass murderer, a person who has abused drugs, someone who has attention deficit disorder, and many more.

Inside the Teenage Brain

www.pbs.org/wgbh/pages/frontline/shows/teenbrain

This site explains teen brain development and how it relates to teen behavior. It describes the individual parts of the brain, from the areas that need sleep and hold memories to the circuitry that makes us emotional beings.

The Secret Life of the Brain

www.pbs.org/wnet/brain/3d/index.html

Learn more about brain functioning at this Public Broadcasting Services Web site. This site enables you to take a 3-D tour through the brain, navigating your way through lobes and ventricles.

HEALTHY LIFESTYLE

About Face

www.about-face.org

Check out the Making Changes section at this Web site, dedicated to empowering teens, for advice on how to improve body image and feel comfortable in your own skin.

American Psychological Association

750 First Street NE

Washington, DC 20002

1-800-374-2721

www.apa.org

The APA is a national organization of psychologists. Go to their Web site to learn more about post-traumatic stress disorder, depression, and many other mental health issues. Click on "Find a psychologist" to find a counselor in your area. Click on "anger" under "psychology topics" to learn more about anger and anger management. That section also offers ways to keep anger under control, gives anger management strategies, and provides advice about when specialized help is needed.

Cool It! Teen Tips to Keep Hot Tempers from Boiling Over by Michael Hershorn (Far Hills, NJ: New Horizon Press, 2003).
This guide helps teens explore the causes of their anger. It also teaches them healthy nonviolent ways to express and manage their feelings through communication and coping methods.

Health World Online
www.healthy.net
This site contains useful health-related information for men and women, as well as teens, on everything from herbal medicine to visualization. It also gives helpful hints on breathing and exercising techniques, ways to improve emotional and physical health, and tips for dealing with stress.

Quick Fixes to Change Your Life: Making Healthy Choices by Judy Ann Walz, M.S.N., R.N. (Midland, GA: Creative Health Services, Inc., 1995).
A helpful book for busy parents and kids that offers tips on stress management and relaxation strategies. It covers topics ranging from sexuality to spirituality to establishing boundaries in school and at work.

TeensHealth
www.teenshealth.org
This Web site addresses many of the questions teens have about their mental and physical health today. It answers questions like, "How much food should I eat?" and addresses hot topics like body piercing and tattoos, cutting, rape, alcohol and drug abuse, and many more! Click on "Your Mind," then on "How Can I Deal with My Anger?" for tips about how to tame anger, as well as a five-step approach to managing frustration. This section also includes advice on when to seek help.

The Wellness Book: The Comprehensive Guide to Maintaining Health and Treating Stress-Related Illness by Herbert Benson, M.D. (New York: Fireside, 1993).

The Wellness Book gives examples and offers a modern take on personal healthcare. It suggests a mind and body connection that can prevent and treat numerous physical and emotional ailments.

RELATIONSHIPS

Bringing Up Parents: The Teenager's Handbook by Alex J. Packer (Minneapolis: Free Spirit Publishing, 1993).

This book gives great tips for how teens can deal with frustration and resolve conflicts within their families. It also provides ideas for ways to improve relationships with parents, as well as pointers for parents about learning to trust and respect their teen.

The Courage to Be Yourself: True Stories by Teens About Cliques, Conflicts, and Overcoming Peer Pressure edited by Al Desetta (Minneapolis: Free Spirit Publishing, 2005).

True, courageous stories from real teens about breaking stereotypes, standing up for what they believe in, and learning who they really are.

The Fourth R
CAMH Centre for Prevention Science
100 Collip Circle, Suite 100
Western Research and Development Park
London, ON N6G 4X8
519-858-5144
www.thefourthr.ca
This organization brings together researchers dedicated to promoting healthy adolescent relationships by helping educators develop the fourth R (relationship) in their schools. They work to improve youth relationships by advocating healthy decisions.

National Domestic Violence Helpline
1-800-799-SAFE (7233)
www.ndvh.org/help/index.html
Males and females who are in violent relationships can call 24 hours a day for free, confidential support, assistance, and services. They offer assistance

in both English and Spanish, and provide intervention, safety planning, and numerous resources for those concerned with personal safety. For more information at the Web site, click "Info for Teens."

Stepfamily Network
www.stepfamily.net
The Stepfamily Network is a Web site created to give teens advice on the best way to deal with stepparents entering their lives. It includes a teen forum and suggestions for numerous books and articles, all showing how teens learned to deal with stepparents.

The Teen Survival Guide to Dating and Relating by Annie Fox (Minneapolis: Free Spirit Publishing, 2005).
This book gives teens advice from both male and female perspectives about relationships, learning to communicate with teachers and parents, finding and trusting friends, and dealing with anger, embarrassment, and other everyday emotions. It also discusses sex and physical risks.

Teen Wire
www.teenwire.com
This teen-specific Web site offers advice on family matters, friendships, relationships, sexual choices, and health. Click "Ask the experts" to get answers from healthcare professionals to your own questions.

MENTAL DISORDERS

The Bipolar Child
www.bipolarchild.com
This site provides published literature about early onset bipolar disorder. Articles and books are updated daily, providing the most current information about this condition.

Child and Adolescent Bipolar Foundation
www.bpkids.org
This parent-led organization educates families, professionals, and the public about pediatric bipolar disorder. Families with children who are diagnosed at an early age with bipolar disorder can connect with each other through membership.

Children and Adults with Attention Deficit/Hyperactivity Disorder (CHADD)

www.chadd.org

This organization is composed of volunteers from around the country, helping individuals and families dealing with ADD or ADHD. The Web site is filled with testimonials and guides to scholastic success, and is an easily accessible resource for education and support.

Covenant House Nineline

1-800-999-9999

www.nineline.org

The Nineline is a free, confidential resource to call or email 24 hours a day, 7 days a week. Counselors and professionals will help answer tough questions regarding separation, divorce, suicide, addiction, health, relationships, abuse, and other issues.

National Association of Anorexia Nervosa and Associated Disorders (ANAD)

847-831-3438

www.anad.org

ANAD works to promote self-acceptance and healthy living. Their helpline (open Monday through Friday 9 AM to 5 PM CST) offers counseling and free support from healthcare professionals. The Web site includes information about eating disorders and treatment referrals for your area.

National Center for Learning Disabilites (NCLD)

212-545-7510

www.ncld.org

The NCLD provides information on learning disabilities and assistance that is available. It helps ensure that students with learning disabilities are given equal opportunities to succeed in school and at work.

National Eating Disorders Association

206-382-3587

www.edap.org

Get info on all forms of eating disorders and treatment, as well as referrals for doctors, counselors, nutritionists, and facilities in your area.

National Hopeline Network

1-800-784-2433

www.hopeline.com

The Kristin Brooks Hope Center provides this suicide prevention hotline, open 24 hours a day, as well as a helpful Web site. They provide information about depression and suicide, as well as journals and other assorted outreach information. The Hopeline Network aims to prevent suicide on a national scale.

National Institute of Mental Health (NIMH)

6001 Executive Boulevard, Room 8184, MSC 9663

Bethesda, MD 20892

866-615-6464

www.nimh.nih.gov

NIMH is a leading federal agency for the research of mental and behavioral disorders. The Web site provides research studies, articles, and other resources. Click "Health Information" to learn more about depression, bipolar disorder, eating disorders, and many other disorders. You'll also find numerous treatment strategies.

When Nothing Matters Anymore: A Survival Guide for Depressed Teens by **Bev Cobain (Minneapolis: Free Spirit Publishing, 2007).**

This book is a helpful guide for teens on how to recognize, understand, and cope with various types of depression. It provides information about how the condition begins, how it can affect a teen's life, and the best ways to seek help.

LAW AND RIGHTS

Juvenile Justice InfoCenter

www.juvenilejusticecenter.com

This Web site contains a wide range of juvenile justice information. You can get help with understanding the law, finding a lawyer, and understanding the variety of lawsuits a person can file.

National Youth Rights Association
301-738-6769
www.youthrights.org
The National Youth Rights Association is dedicated to defending the civil and human rights of young people. Their goal is to educate teens about their rights, while working with public officials to create policy solutions about problems affecting America's youth today.

What Are My Rights? 95 Questions and Answers About Teens and the Law **by Thomas A. Jacobs (Minneapolis: Free Spirit Publishing, 2006).**
This book answers questions about the law, from the simple "Can I have a beer?" to the more difficult, "Can my property be searched and seized?" Teens can learn about how the law affects them on a daily basis, consider their responsibilities as an American citizen, and learn to appreciate their rights.

Amen, D. G. & Routh, L. C. *Healing Anxiety and Depression*. New York: G.P. Putnam's Sons, 2003.

American Psychiatric Association. *Diagnostic and Statistical Manual of Mental Disorders*. Washington, DC: American Psychiatric Association, 2000.

Anderson, C. A. & Dill, K. E. "Video Games and Aggressive Thoughts, Feelings, and Behavior in the Laboratory and in Life." *Journal of Personality and Social Psychology*. 2000, Vol. 78, No. 4, 772–790.

"Angry Young Men Risk Heart Attacks." BBC News, April 22, 2002. Retrieved from http://news.bbc.co.uk/1/hi/health/1939094.stm (March 22, 2006).

Bloomquist, M. L. *Helping Children with Aggression and Conduct Problems*. New York: The Guilford Press, 2002.

Bolick, T. *Asperger Syndrome and Adolescence*. Gloucester, MA: Fair Winds Press, 2001.

"Children's Mental Health Statistics" from Mental Health America. Retrieved from http://www1.nmha.org/children/prevent/stats.cfm (June 28, 2007).

Conterio, K. & Lader, W. *Bodily Harm*. New York: Hyperion, 1998.

Donovan, F. *Dealing with Your Anger*. Alameda, CA: Hunter House Publishers, 1999.

"Fish Is Anger Management Food." National Center for Policy Analysis, April 25, 2006. Retrieved from http://www.ncpa.org/newdpd/dpdarticle. php?article_id=3240 (June 28, 2007).

"Fish Oil Supplements May Reduce Anger." *Nutrition Industry Executive*, March 2006. Retrieved from http://www.europasports.com/flextime/ content/industry/omega3_reduces_anger.cfm (June 28, 2007).

Golden, B. *Healthy Anger*. New York: Oxford University Press, Inc., 2003.

Goleman, D. *Emotional Intelligence.* New York: Bantam Books, 1995.

Gottlieb, M. M. *The Angry Self.* Phoenix, AZ: Zeig, Tucker & Co., 1999.

Gottman, John M. *The Marriage Clinic: A Scientifically-Based Marital Therapy.* New York: W. W. Norton & Company, 1999.

Hedaya, R. J. *Understanding Biological Psychiatry.* New York: W. W. Norton & Company, 1996.

Henderson, K. "Overview of ADA, IDEA, and Section 504." KidSourceOnline. Retrieved from http://www.kidsource.com/kidsource/content3/ada.idea.html (June 28, 2007).

Jacobs, T. A. *What Are My Rights?* Minneapolis: Free Spirit Publishing, 2006.

"Juvenile Crime." From the Office of Juvenile Justice and Delinquency Prevention (ND). Retrieved from http://www.juvenilejusticefyi.com/juvenile_crimes.html (June 28, 2007).

"Juvenile Offenders." Virginia Commission on Youth, 2003. Retrieved from http://coy.state.va.us/Modalities/juvoffenders.htm (July 3, 2007).

Kassinove, H. & Tafrate, R. C. *Anger Management.* Atascadero, CA: Impact Publishers, Inc., 2002.

LeDoux, J. *The Emotional Brain.* New York: Touchstone, 1996.

Luecke, D. L. *The Relationship Manual.* Columbia, MD: The Relationship Institute, 1981.

McKay, M. & Rogers, P. *The Anger Control Workbook.* Oakland, CA: New Harbinger Publications, Inc., 2000.

"The Numbers Count: Mental Illness in America." National Institute of Mental Health, December 26, 2006. Retrieved from http://www.nimh.nih.gov/publicat/numbers.cfm#Intro (July 3, 2007).

"Omega-3 Fatty Acids." The University of Maryland Medical Center, 2006. Retrieved from http://www.umm.edu/altmed/ConsSupplements/Omega3FattyAcidscs.html (June 28, 2007).

Paleg, K. & McKay, M. *When Anger Hurts Your Relationship*. Oakland, CA: New Harbinger Publications, Inc., 2001.

Potter-Efron, R. & Potter-Efron, P. *Letting Go of Anger*. Oakland, CA: New Harbinger Publications, Inc., 1995.

Simmer, S. C. *Vicious Circles Manual: Anger Management for Men*. Northampton, MA: Reach Educational Seminars, 1999.

Tebartz van Elst, L., Woermann, F. G., Lemieux, L., Thompson, P. J., & Trimble, M. R. "Affective aggression in patients with temporal lobe epilepsy." *Brain* (2000), 123, 234–243. Retrieved from http://brain.oxfordjournals.org/cgi/reprint/123/2/234 (April 30, 2006).

Wallis, C. & Dell, K. "What Makes Teens Tick." *Time,* May 10, 2004, Vol. 163, No. 19.

Wells, V. *The Joy of Visualization*. San Francisco, CA: Chronicle Books, 1990.

Williams, R. & Williams, V. *Anger Kills*. New York: HarperCollins Publishers, Inc., 1993.

James J. Crist, Ph.D., CSAC, is a licensed clinical psychologist and a certified substance abuse counselor with the Child and Family Counseling Center in Woodbridge, Virginia. He works with a wide variety of clients, including children, adolescents, adults, couples, and families. He specializes in working with attention disorders, depression, bipolar disorder, anxiety disorders, and drug and alcohol abuse. He is also an adjunct faculty member in the professional counseling program at Argosy University. Dr. Crist is a graduate of Williams College in Massachusetts and the University of North Carolina at Chapel Hill, where he earned his Ph.D. in clinical psychology. This is his sixth book.

Other Great Books from Free Spirit!